P9-DBL-841

AUTOBIOGRAPHY OF BENJAMIN FRANKLIN

NOTES

including
- *Introduction*
- *Brief Summary*
- *Summaries and Discussions*
- *Critical Analysis*
- *Character Sketches*
- *Study Questions*
- *Bibliography*

by
Merrill Maguire Skaggs, Ph.D.

Cliffs Notes

INCORPORATED

LINCOLN, NEBRASKA   68501

Editor

Gary Carey, M.A.
University of Colorado

Consulting Editor

James L. Roberts, Ph.D.
Department of English
University of Nebraska

CONTENTS

INTRODUCTION

Benjamin Franklin, 1706–1790, printer, scientist, states-man, wrote an *Autobiography* which poses a riddle never completely solved: How could such an incomplete, disjointed, inaccurate, mangled manuscript be so perennially popular? Trans-lated into dozens of languages and reprinted in hundreds of editions, it continues to be one of the most successful books of all time, even though Franklin himself is sometimes viewed with suspicion by the haters of industry and frugality. An an-swer to the riddle of the *Autobiography* is partially hinted at by the ways in which it has been described, for if it has not been all things to all men, it has at least been remarkable to most men who have read it. Its most admired qualities have changed as fashions, philosophies, and needs have changed. But, signifi-cantly, the book continues to survive such changes.

For the diminishing numbers interested in obtaining moral instruction through their entertainment—a group including an apparent majority of nineteenth-century readers—Franklin's *Autobiography* is indeed a prize. His friends had urged him to complete his story in order to direct young people in the ways they should go; and it was primarily as a moral tract that expur-gated versions of the *Autobiography* were first taught in Ameri-can schools. Less didactic historians, however, have found the book equally valuable as the first detailed study of the American middle-class, a map of the road to wealth which that WASPish congregation traveled after secularizing their Protestant ener-gies. Still others have seen it as a revolutionary document—an assertion of proletarian dignity and the tangible portrayal of a mind confident enough to seek new forms of government.

For those uninterested in questions of history or morality, the *Autobiography* gratifies the longing for a success story, for

5

a book about a virtuous hero who survives many trials and makes good. Indeed, the *Autobiography* just begins to hint of the astonishing triumphs in store for Franklin before his death. Long before his years of public service were over he had been referred to in Parliament as one of the wisest men of Europe, and had been courted by kings.

During his 1764–1775 term as colonial agent in England, Franklin was considered by the British the quintessential American. Later, in France, he seemed to romantics an ideal—a noble savage miraculously comfortable at court. His character indicated to Europeans just what the provinces could produce. Many have therefore valued his *Autobiography* for the insight it affords into the mind of an American leader, a Founding Father, and for the picture of life in colonial America which it provides. And those interested in dissecting the components of the American character have perforce studied Franklin's *Autobiography*, if only because the reverence with which it was viewed made it a shaping influence on American thought.

Finally, for those uninterested in history, personality, or colonial sociology, there is still the language of the *Autobiography* to admire. When other considerations fade, Franklin is the master of the well-turned phrase, the succinctly pointed anecdote, the balanced sentence, humanized with an undercurrent of wry, sophisticated, self-critical, and ironic wit.

How the Autobiography Was Written

In 1771, when Franklin was sixty-five years old and had been serving in England seven years as Agent for Pennsylvania (his second stay in this capacity), he visited for two weeks at the home of Jonathan Shipley, Bishop of St. Asaph, at Twyford. As part of his vacation, he outlined the story of his life and then wrote eighty-six pages, bringing his account up to 1730. But the leisurely rest at Twyford ended and he laid his *Memoirs,* as he called the *Autobiography,* aside, not to return to them for thirteen years. He had carried his story only up to the point at which he began to be locally prominent in Philadelphia. (This section, which for convenience scholars call Part One, covers, in the following synopses, Sections 1–7.)

The intervening years, before Franklin began to write about himself again, were turbulent ones, encompassing the American

Revolution. Almost as soon as the Declaration of Independence was signed, the American Congress sent Franklin as its Commissioner to France. While living just outside Paris at Passy, Franklin began Part Two (Sections 8 and 9 here) of his story in 1784, when he was over seventy-eight years old. But he found time to pen only seventeen pages before he laid the work aside again for four more years.

Increasingly ill with gout and gallstones, Franklin was finally allowed to return to America, but had no sooner arrived than he was elected President of Pennsylvania and then Delegate to the Federal Convention of 1787. Thus he found himself once more too busy with public affairs to indulge in personal reminiscences. But in July, 1788, he made his will, and in August began his *Memoirs* again, this time writing one hundred and seventeen pages (Sections 10–17). Franklin was now eighty-three, and so constantly in pain that he had to resort to opium for respite. Sometime before his death on April 17, 1790, at the age of eighty-four, he wrote his last seven and one-half pages, comprising what scholars call Part Four (Section 18).

Publication History of the Autobiography

For writing usually characterized by simplicity and clarity, Franklin's *Autobiography* comes to us with an extraordinarily complicated and murky publishing history. When he returned from England in 1775, Franklin brought with him the unrevised manuscript of Part One. He left it, along with other important papers, in the care of a friend, Joseph Galloway, when Congress sent him to France in 1776. But Galloway sided with the British during the Revolution and therefore had to flee from Philadelphia when the British troops withdrew. His wife stayed to protect their home, but died soon thereafter, apparently leaving the manuscript of Franklin's *Autobiography* in the hands of her executor, Abel James, a lawyer. James then wrote Franklin urging him to continue the story and sending him his original outline of proposed topics.

One mystery about the manuscript begins brewing while only Part One exists, hypothetically in James's possession as executor of Mrs. Galloway's will: later unauthorized editions of Part One are easiest explained by supposing that one of James's clerks stealthily made a copy of it while it was still in James's office, and that the secret copy somehow got to England immediately after Franklin's death.

While in France, Franklin was visited by his close friend Benjamin Vaughan, who had been sent by the British government to discuss peace negotiations. Franklin showed Vaughan James's letter, asking his opinion of it, and Vaughan found even more reasons than James had for urging Franklin to continue. Both letters are inserted at the beginning of Part Two, apparently to explain why Franklin continued to write after being estranged from his son William Temple, for whom the *Memoirs* were planned originally.

When Franklin, back in Philadelphia, finally began writing again in 1788, he apparently reread and probably revised his draft of Part One. Then he had his grandson, Benjamin Franklin Bache, make two copies of his first three parts and sent them to Benjamin Vaughan in England and to his friend Le Veillard in France, asking them for their suggestions and comments. At this point another mystery is born, for we have no way of knowing to what extent Franklin personally authorized the many changes in Bache's copies, and to what extent they were editorial corrections Bache himself supplied. To complicate matters further, though the first authorized edition of the *Autobiography* was based on one of Bache's copies, neither copy survives today. The exact wording of Bache's versions must be reconstructed from printed editions of the book and from translations supposedly based on Bache's copies rather than the original manuscript.

Le Veillard began translating the *Autobiography* into French as soon as he received one of Bache's copies. He proceeded meticulously, attempting to render as exactly as possible Franklin's English expressions and comparisons into French. But Franklin, after adding the last short section before his death, left the publication rights for the book to his illegitimate grandson, William Temple Franklin, Jr. And Temple, hoping to make a great deal of money out of a book for which the public was clamoring, forbade its publication in English or French, except in authorized editions which he himself would edit. But Temple found working from the original manuscript difficult, since the handwriting was often illegible, so at some point he apparently exchanged manuscripts with Le Veillard, taking to his printer Bache's neater copy to use, and failing to notice that

Part Four had been added at the end of the original. He did not bring out his edition until 1818.

Within a year after Franklin's death in 1790, an un-authorized French translation of Part One appeared, followed two years later by London editions which were supposedly unauthorized re-translations into English from the poor French translation. Several mysteries arise because of these works: first, from what possible text was the French translation made (Le Veillard convincingly denied having anything to do with it); and second, what sources were used for the English re-transla-tions, since occasional wordings resemble the original manu-script more than the supposed French source? The simplest explanation is that all these pirated editions were taken from a copy of Part One made in Abel James's office.

Le Veillard died on the scaffold during the French Revolu-tion, and Temple Franklin dawdled so in publishing Franklin's papers that gossips suggested he had been bribed by the British government to suppress them. But finally he brought out the first three parts of the *Autobiography* in 1818, the text based on Bache's copy. Years later, in 1868, the American minister to France, John Bigelow, located and brought from Le Veillard's heirs the original manuscript. He then noted how widely it differed from the official edition and brought out what he claimed was the definitive edition of the *Autobiography,* in the process reviling Temple Franklin on a number of grounds. But since Bigelow simply made corrections on a printed copy of the Temple Franklin edition, his own "definitive edition" has as many errors as he claimed the original definitive edition contained.

Temple Franklin was unjustly accused of bowdlerizing his grandfather's powerful prose. Of course, since neither of Bache's copies exists, it is impossible to know for sure what changes each grandson contributed in the 1818 version. But neither can any-one know whether many of these changes were not made by Franklin himself, when he directed Bache's copying. Conse-quently, no absolutely foolproof and totally authoritative text representing Franklin's final wishes will probably ever exist.

What Happened After the Autobiography Ends

In many ways, Franklin's *Autobiography* stops when it

approaches the period of activity which made such memoirs most desirable. Although his scientific and philosophical reputations were based largely on the electrical experiments he mentions briefly in the *Autobiography,* his most significant political contributions were made after 1758, when the *Memoirs* ended. Considering both aspects of his career, Turgot coined for Franklin the Latin motto *Eripuit caelo fulmen sceptrumque tyrannis:* "He snatched the lightning from the sky and the scepter from tyrants."

Franklin's first mission to England to negotiate about the taxes which the Pennsylvania Proprietors refused to pay lasted from 1757 to 1762. During this time Franklin, with his son William, visited the homes of their ancestors, as Franklin reminded William at the beginning of the *Autobiography,* and in 1759 was awarded an honorary Doctor of Laws degree from the University of St. Andrews. Thereafter he was addressed as "Dr. Franklin." On this trip he spent an extended time in Scotland, with many intellectual luminaries then living around Edinburgh, and called the visit "six weeks of the *densest* happiness I have met with in any part of my life." He was later given a doctor's degree by Oxford, and had the satisfaction of seeing his son William, who had accompanied him on most of his official missions to this point, appointed governor of New Jersey. He also continued his experiments and perfected a musical instrument called the armonica, which involved glasses filled with varying amounts of water and played with a wet finger rubbed round the rims. The instrument was so popular that Mozart and Beethoven, as well as others, composed music for it.

Franklin arrived home in Philadelphia on November 1, 1762, settled hopefully into domestic routine, prepared to serve as an Assembly member, and began to build a new house for his family. But in early winter of the following year he was again embroiled in public controversy. Frontiersmen, inflamed by Indian uprisings, killed two groups of friendly Indians; and Franklin wrote a pamphlet strongly condemning this massacre. The same settlers then decided to march on Philadelphia to murder the friendly Indians being guarded there. But Franklin met them outside the city, talked with them, reminded them of the three companies of soldiers defending Philadelphia, and persuaded them to go home without causing further trouble.

At this point bitterness increased against the Proprietors, who controlled Pennsylvania under Royal charters inherited from William Penn. A faction led by Franklin convinced a majority of the Assembly to petition the King to take direct control of the Province. Opponents argued that the King's representatives would govern as corruptly as the Proprietors' men, and that to lose the Proprietors would be to lose the excellent Pennsylvania charter. Franklin's allies won the vote to petition the King, but on October 1, 1764, after a bitter and vituperative campaign, Franklin lost his seat in the Assembly. By the end of the month, however, the Assembly discovered that it could not do without his services and voted to send him again to England in order to present their petition. Again his wife Deborah refused to sail across the ocean, so he left without her. He was never to see her again, for he was unable to return for ten more years; and before he arrived, Deborah died.

When Franklin arrived in England as Colonial agent for the second time, his purpose was to end Proprietary government in Pennsylvania. Since he was later appointed agent for Georgia in 1768, New Jersey in 1769, and Massachusetts in 1770, however, he came to be regarded as the representative for all the American colonies. As the breach between England and the Colonies widened, Franklin began to be feared and hated as the embodiment of selfish American demands.

Over Franklin's opposition, the Stamp Act decreeing that stamps must be placed on all official documents was passed on March 22, 1765, as a method of bringing revenue into the British treasury. Since the American Assemblies claimed as a primary right the privilege of taxing themselves, the Americans were outraged. Franklin unwisely recommended his friends as distributors of the stamps and so was suspected of framing the act himself. But he worked tirelessly for its repeal, his labors given more leverage by American riots and boycotts of English goods. The climax of his struggle came on February 13, 1766, with Franklin's brilliant performance before Parliament (partially arranged beforehand) in which he answered the members' questions and explained the American position. The whole transcript of his examination was published in England, France, and throughout the Colonies, making Franklin the major colonial hero of the day. A month later he received most of the credit when the unpopular Stamp Act was repealed by Parliament.

In the years which followed, Franklin apparently remained hopeful that a stable and powerful British Empire could be formed. But relations were slowly deteriorating between the American colonies and England. Franklin wrote newspaper articles explaining the American position and, when those failed to work, wrote several brilliant satires and hoaxes attacking the British government. While these cutting satires may have affected public opinion, making some of the British more sympathetic to the Americans, they certainly embittered the officials of the government. Inevitably, such men found a way to revenge themselves upon their troublesome American gadfly.

On December 2, 1772, Franklin had sent secretly to a committee of the Massachusetts Assembly a group of letters he had been given, which were written by the Governor of Massachusetts, Thomas Hutchinson, and the Lieutenant-Governor, Andrew Oliver. Both men urged English officials to make stronger and better enforced demands on the colonists as a means of suppressing rebellious American spirits. Against Franklin's wishes, the letters were eventually published and aroused an impassioned public demand that the Governor be removed from office. In the ensuing furor, Franklin admitted having sent the letters to Hutchinson's enemies. On January 29, 1774, Franklin was called before the Privy Council, excoriated publicly in the most excessive style, accused of stealing the letters and of plotting against representatives of the Crown, and denounced for nearly an hour, to the glee of the applauding audience. He stood silently and refused to answer. Two days later he was removed from his office of deputy postmaster general.

Obviously Franklin could no longer work openly and effectively with the British government. There is evidence that by the end of the year various officials were again attempting to contact him, because he was the only man considered capable of engineering a satisfactory compromise with the increasingly angry colonies. But by this time the positions of the colonies and the mother country were virtually irreconcilable. Hope for a settlement flared briefly when William Pitt, Lord Chatham, presented a plan Franklin liked to the House of Lords. But the Lords rejected it and launched an insulting personal attack on

Franklin, who was in the audience. Franklin finally gave up all hope of a peaceful settlement and sailed for Philadelphia in March, 1775.

He landed at Philadelphia on May 5 and on May 6 was elected as delegate to the Second Continental Congress. The rest of 1775 was spent working endlessly on the numerous committees to which he was appointed (work which included reviewing Jefferson's draft of the Declaration of Independence). At the age of seventy, he became a fervent revolutionary, proving his ardor by loaning the new Congress all the money he could personally raise, thereby encouraging others to do the same and aiding immeasurably the new government's finances.

In the autumn of 1776 Congress appointed Franklin one of three commissioners to the court of France. He quickly sailed to Europe on a warship, the capture of which would have meant his immediate execution by the British as a traitor. But once in Paris he was lionized, indeed idolized, by an adoring French public. His enormous personal prestige gave him more power than any other American could have wielded in negotiations with the French government. And by playing on the French desire to see the British Empire diminished, Franklin wheedled from the absolute monarchy of Louis XVI the funds which enabled the Colonies to successfully defend the independence they had declared. Though he was surrounded with British spies and American enemies, the latter either jealous of his adulation or disapproving of his courtly methods, Franklin traced in his French years one of the most successful diplomatic careers of the American foreign service. The period culminated with his personal direction of the negotiations for peace with England, and with the signing of the peace treaty on September 3, 1783. Franklin was officially replaced by Thomas Jefferson on May 2, 1785, and left his French home July 12, carried in one of the Queen's personal litters to spare him unnecessary pain from his gallstones.

Franklin landed in Philadelphia on September 14, 1785, greeted by cannon salutes, cheering crowds, and public celebrations befitting the arrival of America's most illustrious citizen. In October he was elected a member, and later president, of the Supreme Executive Council of Pennsylvania, and began another phase of his public service. From May through September of

1787 he also served as one of Pennsylvania's delegates to the Constitutional Convention. Though virtually none of his ideas were incorporated into the document this Convention eventually adopted, he has been convincingly credited with holding the warring factions together in order to work out the compromise structure that was eventually ratified. His last speech urging unanimous acceptance of the compromise was reprinted over fifty times as arguments about ratification raged throughout the Colonies: "I confess that there are several parts of this Constitution which I do not at present approve, but I am not sure I shall never approve them. . . . Though many . . . persons think . . . highly of their own infallibility . . . , few express it so naturally as a certain French lady, who . . . said, 'I don't know how it happens, sister, but I meet with nobody but myself that is always in the right. . . .' I cannot help expressing a wish that every member of the Convention . . . would with me, on this occasion, doubt a little of his own infallibility, and, to make manifest our unanimity, put his name to this instrument."

When Franklin ended his term as president of Pennsylvania's Supreme Executive Council in October, 1788, his public career was finally finished. He spent the last two years of his life in "excruciating Pain," but wrote President Washington, "I am pleas'd that I have liv'd them, since they have brought me to see our present Situation." His last public act was to sign a congressional petition advocating the abolition of slavery. Then on an April evening in 1790, at the age of 84, Benjamin Franklin quietly died.

BRIEF SUMMARY OF THE AUTOBIOGRAPHY

Benjamin Franklin was the youngest son and fifteenth of seventeen children of Josiah Franklin, a soap and candle maker who had immigrated to Boston from Northamptonshire, England. Because he disliked his father's trade but loved reading, he was apprenticed at the age of twelve to his brother James, a printer. He and James often disagreed, and finally Benjamin quit before his contract had expired. Looking for work, he went first to New York and then to Philadelphia, where he was hired by Samuel Keimer.

Governor Keith of Pennsylvania was impressed with

Franklin and offered to set him up in business. Assuming that Keith had placed letters of credit for him on board his ship, Franklin sailed for England to purchase his printing equipment, only to find that no such letters had been written. He therefore was forced to spend several months working in a London printing house. But he returned home when a merchant named Denham offered him a good job as clerk and manager of Denham's Philadelphia store. A few months after they landed, however, Denham died, and Keimer rehired Franklin as his manager.

Eventually Franklin set up a printing shop with one of the men he had trained at Keimer's, Hugh Meredith. Later he bought Meredith's share and found himself in business alone. He "married" the girl whom he had courted before leaving for England, Deborah Read, and the two prospered. Franklin secured many valuable orders through his job as clerk of the Pennsylvania Assembly.

From his early years, Franklin constantly struggled to improve himself. This passion culminated in a plan to attain perfection in thirteen weeks, by unlearning bad habits and acquiring the thirteen virtues Franklin felt most important, one each week. He also outlined a perfect day, alloting each necessary activity its proper amount of time.

But Franklin's passion for improvement was not spent exclusively upon himself. Public projects to which he turned his attention included Philadelphia's first public library, fire company, public academy, philosophical society, militia, defense system, and hospital. Besides these projects, he helped improve the city's police system and its streets (which he advocated paving), and devised a more equitable tax system.

The *Autobiography* ends as Franklin wins his first skirmish while serving as Pennsylvania's agent in England. Thus his account brings the reader to the point at which Franklin's activity becomes international in scope and the proper concern of professional historians.

NOTE: This guide divides the *Autobiography* into sections for the convenience of the reader.

SUMMARIES
AND DISCUSSIONS

PART ONE
SECTION 1

SYNOPSIS: Franklin's Family Background

Franklin begins by stating five reasons for writing his autobiography. First, since he has always enjoyed anecdotes about his ancestors, he hopes his own life story will interest his son. Second, since he was a poor boy who found fame and fortune, he hopes his story will provide others with a good model to imitate. Third, since he can't relive his life as he would like to do, he will relive it through memories, and by recording the memories, make his life durable. Fourth, his writing will allow him to reminisce without boring any listeners. And fifth, his account will gratify his vanity.

He first sketches a brief family history. The English Franklins lived for as far back as records went in the same Northamptonshire village, on their thirty-acre property. Benjamin's grandfather Thomas had four sons, the eldest of whom, also named Thomas, followed the family trade as a blacksmith, and was also a scrivener (a scribe and notary), and a public leader. John and Benjamin, the two middle sons, were trained as dyers, though Benjamin, his namesake records, was also a poet, politician, and inventor of a shorthand system. Josiah, the youngest of these four brothers, emigrated to Boston with a group seeking greater religious freedom. Josiah had seventeen children by two wives, and named his youngest son Benjamin, after his brother.

Young Benjamin's parents were both religious. His mother, Abiah Folger, came from a devout family of early New England settlers, while the Franklins had been known in England for their Protestant steadfastness. Josiah Franklin planned that Benjamin should be a clergyman, the "tithe" of his sons. To prepare him for this vocation, Josiah sent Benjamin to grammar school for a year, but withdrew him after deciding that a clergyman's training was too expensive, especially since ministers were often

16

so poorly paid. Instead, Benjamin was sent to a writing and arithmetic school where he failed arithmetic twice (though he later learned it on his own). But after two years of formal schooling, ten-year-old Benjamin was brought home to help in the family business of making candles and soap.

Young Franklin disliked the chandler's trade and longed to go to sea. He excelled in water sports, but once led several playmates into trouble because of such pastimes. He persuaded the boys to steal some large stones amassed to build a new house, and use them instead for a fishing wharf. When reprimanded by his father, young Ben defended himself by pleading that he had made something practical. But his father convinced him that "nothing was useful which was not honest."

Ben's father, Josiah Franklin, who lived to the age of eighty-nine, was talented at drawing, music, and mechanical tasks, and was publicly recognized for his excellent judgment. At mealtime, for example, he provided conversation to instruct his children. The family paid little attention to food, a habit Franklin found advantageous when he later traveled extensively without ever feeling inconvenienced by poor fare.

Since Josiah feared young Benjamin would run away to sea if made to continue in the family trade, the father and son walked together around Boston to see "Joiners, Bricklayers, Turners, Braziers" at work and to observe what kind of task most appealed to the boy. Franklin felt this experience was most useful to him later, since it taught him how to do little jobs for himself, how to construct the machines he would later use for his experiments, and how to admire a workman doing his job well. Finally, because of Benjamin's love of reading, Josiah apprenticed him to his brother James, a printer.

DISCUSSION

From the first line, Franklin's *Autobiography* illustrates the complex character of the man who wrote it, not only through the facts it states but also through the attitudes it reveals. The productive tension in Franklin's nature between the light-hearted and the earnest is evident by the end of the first paragraph. While Franklin starts his account as a paternal (and presumably chatty) letter to his son, he soon begins the formal statement about his worthy purposes—the rationalizations for the work to follow—which one expects of highly serious eight-eenth-century treatises. But after presenting three respectable reasons for writing, Franklin appends two frivolous ones, and by doing so gently mocks the literary conventions he follows. Thus from the beginning we glimpse a man who accepts reasonable and recognized rules, but keeps a playful spirit alive while doing so.

QUESTION

What elements of Franklin's family tradition and upbringing help partially to explain the man's later versatility and achievements?

SECTION 2

SYNOPSIS: The Apprentice

At the age of twelve, Benjamin reluctantly signed an indenture contract, to work without pay (except for his last year of service) until he was twenty-one. But he learned his printing-house duties quickly, and much more besides. From friends apprenticed to booksellers, he was able to borrow books which he read throughout many nights. And under the encouragement of his brother, he learned to compose ballads about local topics and peddle them successfully around the streets. His father made fun of the verses, and discouraged Benjamin from writing poetry, since poets usually made so poor a living.

Most important, however, Benjamin learned at this time to write effective prose. His lessons began when he engaged in a running, written argument with his friend John Collins about the plausibility of educating women, a scheme Franklin favored. When Benjamin's father read the letters and pointed out that his son's writing lacked elegance and clarity, Benjamin resolved to improve it. First he tried imitating the *Spectator* papers. He would jot down the ideas of articles, then after a few days write the ideas out in his own sentences, which he would compare with the originals. He wrote verse in order to increase his awareness of words, and turned stories into verse and back again in order to gain writing practice. He would also jumble an essay's state-

ments, then after several weeks try unscrambling them to increase his sense of structure.

When sixteen, Benjamin became a vegetarian and volunteered to board himself for half what his brother was currently
paying. He soon found that by eating frugally, he could save
half the amount his brother gave him, and could use the money
to buy books. Then while his brother and the other apprentices
were eating, he could use the extra time for study.

One book which influenced the boy at this time was an
English rhetoric which included an illustration of "the Socratic
Method." Charmed by Socrates' approach to conversation, Benjamin began to practice drawing people out as Socrates had done,
avoiding any direct contradictions of their opinions. He soon
grew adept at trapping his opponent through ostensibly irrele-
vant questions. He pretended to be "the humble Enquirer and
Doubter," and found the method particularly good in religious
arguments. Though he stopped using this method after awhile,
he always tried to express himself with Socrates' "modest Diffi-
dence," for he found the manner convinced others to follow his
wishes far better than dogmatic assertiveness.

Around 1720 Benjamin's brother began to print a newspaper called the *New England Courant*. Young Benjamin secretly contributed articles which were praised by James's friends,
and thought to be the work of some prominent citizen. When
Benjamin announced himself the author, however, James decided that the praise would make his apprentice conceited.

The two brothers did not get along. Benjamin particularly
resented James's beatings. After James was imprisoned for a
month because of a newspaper article offensive to the Assembly,
however, Benjamin printed in the *Courant* several remarks
which were critical of the government. So when James was re-
leased, he was ordered to stop printing his newspaper. James
decided to circumvent this injunction by making Benjamin the
official printer. But because Benjamin could not serve legally
while he was his brother's apprentice, the two agreed that
Benjamin's contract would be returned publicly, a private agreement on the old terms to be substituted in secret. Soon an argument allowed Benjamin to take advantage of his brother's public
act by refusing to work for him. In effect, he cheated James of
four years of free labor, an act Benjamin later declared "one of

the first Errata of my Life." James's revenge was to prevent Benjamin from getting a job at any other printing-house in Boston.

At this point, Benjamin decided to try his luck in New York, the nearest town boasting printers. Since he could get no work, had made political enemies in the Assembly, and had been labeled an atheist in the town, he felt it judicious to leave Boston. But he feared that his father might prevent his leaving, because he was only seventeen; so he slipped away secretly, telling a ship's captain that he was fleeing friends of a girl he had got pregnant but did not wish to marry.

DISCUSSION

In this section and throughout the *Autobiography,* Franklin takes an understandable pride in his own accomplishments, and an unapologetic stance about his faults. He gives God conventional perfunctory thanks for leading him to his successes, but never professes that he was unworthy of the blessings Providence gave him. If God led him to the means he used for achieving success, Franklin makes clear, those means were still fashioned by his own ingenuity. The point suggests a fact about Franklin which one must remember in order to understand the man's astonishing range of achievements: above all, Franklin accepted himself gladly, believing himself capable of grasping any good thing, if he worked hard enough for it. And this acceptance of himself included not only his talents but also his flaws. His mistakes he calls, significantly, his "errata," a printer's term for typographical errors. The choice of words indicates that Franklin did not think in terms of sins, or moral lapses, or personal inadequacies. Rather, he found some past actions, when considered objectively and impersonally, to be unfortunate deviations from the popular standard. As the *Autobiography* goes on to point out, Franklin felt that many of his errata were later cancelled by other actions which fairly compensated for them. Though he seemed to regret not being perfect from the beginning (and later formulated a scheme for arriving at perfection in thirteen weeks), he apparently wasted little energy agonizing over irremediable mistakes.

QUESTION

How did Benjamin try to improve himself while he was still an indentured apprentice?

SECTION 3

SYNOPSIS: The Arrival in Philadelphia

In New York, Benjamin applied for work to a printer, William Bradford, who advised him to go to Philadelphia, where Bradford's son Andrew, also a printer, had recently lost his helper; so Benjamin started by boat to travel the hundred miles to Philadelphia. On the way, a squall tore up sails and drove Benjamin's boat off course. A drunk Dutchman fell overboard, and Franklin had to fish him out of the water. Unable to land on Long Island, the passengers had to sleep in the boat all night, drenching wet, without food to eat or water to drink. Finally safe in Amboy the next day, Franklin grew feverish, but drank plenty of water and sweated his fever away through the night, then proceeded toward Burlington, fifty miles away, by foot. By noon he was rain-soaked, exhausted, and uncomfortably aware that people suspected him of being a runaway. At Burlington, Franklin sighted a boat going to Philadelphia and caught a ride, but then had to row all the way, besides spending a cold night on the river bank.

When finally a dirty, tired, and hungry Benjamin arrived at Philadelphia on Sunday morning, he had only a Dutch dollar and a copper shilling left. He gave the shilling to the boat owners with whom he had rowed up the river, and later observed that a man is "sometimes more generous when he has but a little Money than when he has plenty, perhaps thro' Fear of being thought to have but little." He found his way to a bakery and, the bread being different from that sold in Boston, asked for three pennies-worth of any kind of bread. Given three great puffy rolls, he had no choice but to carry one under each arm and the third in his hands to eat. So he strolled through the streets, passing his future wife who thought he made "a most awkward ridiculous Appearance." He followed some cleanly-dressed people into the Quaker meeting house but slept through the service until someone woke him at the end. So the first house in Philadelphia he either entered or slept in was the church. After the service, he found respectable accommodations and slept all day and night, waking only to eat at mealtime.

On Monday morning Benjamin visited the printer Bradford and found that Bradford's father had arrived by horseback. So William Bradford of New York was able to introduce Franklin properly to his son. The son had already hired a helper, but suggested that Franklin contact a rival printer, and offered to board him until he should find work. Then, escorted by old Bradford, Franklin went to meet his future employer. The new printer, Keimer, promised Franklin work, but made a bad impression by indiscreetly discussing his business with Mr. Bradford, not realizing that the old man was his rival's father. Franklin discovered that Keimer owned only the most outworn equipment. Furthermore, he was composing an elegy directly into type as he devised verses in his head. Both Philadelphia printers appeared to Benjamin to be unequipped for their profession, since Bradford was "very illiterate," and Keimer knew nothing of how to run a press. Keimer disliked his employee's living at his rival's house, so he arranged for Franklin to move into the Read home, where Benjamin met his future wife.

Franklin's brother-in-law, Captain Robert Holmes (Homes), master of a sloop trading between Boston and Delaware, landed forty miles from Philadelphia, heard of Benjamin's whereabouts, and wrote urging him to return home. Answering, Franklin defended his leaving Boston, and Holmes showed the letter to Sir William Keith, Governor of the Province. Keith was impressed and stated that so promising a young man should be encouraged to begin a printing business in Philadelphia, where he would soon receive all the public business of the Assembly. One day Keith and a friend knocked on Keimer's door and asked for Franklin, whom they invited to accompany them to a nearby tavern. Over Madeira, the two encouraged Benjamin to set up his own business, and promised him their aid. Keith also offered to write a letter asking Benjamin's father to back the proposed printing shop financially. So Franklin decided to return to Boston on the first boat, in the meantime keeping his plans secret but dining occasionally with the governor.

DISCUSSION

Franklin states why he gives the details about his difficult journey to Philadelphia and his disreputable-looking appearance when entering the city: "I have been the more particular in this

Description of my Journey, and shall be so of my first Entry into that City, that you may in your mind compare such unlikely Beginnings with the Figure I have since made there." One factor in the earlier figure as well as that later figure Franklin cut, to which he fails to give just due, is his unusual personal presence which apparently could favorably impress others almost immediately. Though Sir William Keith, the most dramatic example in this section, began to champion Franklin after encountering him only through a letter, the passage abounds with references to people, both humble and proud, who seemed to love Franklin on first sight. William Bradford of New York, a complete stranger, was enough impressed with young Benjamin to undertake the arduous trip to Philadelphia at least partially on Franklin's behalf. Bradford's son Andrew immediately offered the unknown arrival a home until he should get a job. Franklin mentions at length an innkeeper he encountered on his walk to Burlington, Dr. Brown, who so enjoyed Franklin's conversation that he remained Franklin's lifelong friend. At Burlington, where he did not even stop the night, Franklin struck up a warm friendship with an old woman who offered him food and lodging for three days until he could catch a boat to Philadelphia. And Keimer, whom Franklin says repeatedly was a suspicious and jealous man, hired Benjamin by the end of their initial interview. Though Franklin gives this magnetic charm little credit for his steady rise, it partially explains why others always seemed eager to help him.

QUESTION

What personal qualities besides charm seem most evident in Franklin during his journey to Philadelphia?

SECTION 4

SYNOPSIS: A Young Man about Town

In April of 1724, carrying a flattering letter about himself from Governor Keith, Franklin sailed to Boston, ostensibly to visit friends. His appearance delighted his family, which had not heard from him for seven months. His brother James resented his new suit, new watch, and ample pocket money, however, and complained that Benjamin had humiliated him by a display of affluence before the workmen. Franklin's father felt that Governor Keith must lack judgment to think of setting so young a lad up in business, and refused to provide the necessary money, though he did promise to supplement the amount Benjamin could save by living frugally until he was twenty-one. Though Benjamin was unable to secure his father's backing, he at least left Boston with his blessing.

On the trip back, Franklin's boat stopped at Newport, Rhode Island. Here Benjamin visited his brother John, through whom he met a man named Vernon, who asked him to collect a debt in Pennsylvania. He also met two young women and a Quaker lady who came aboard the boat at Newport. But the Quaker warned Benjamin against the other two women, to his later relief; for when the boat docked at New York, where the ladies had invited Benjamin to visit them, the Captain missed some goods, had the lodgings of the two searched, and found the stolen articles there. Benjamin felt lucky to have escaped involvement with them.

While in Boston, Franklin had talked so enthusiastically of Philadelphia that his friend John Collins decided to return with him, and started out by land to meet Benjamin in New York. But when Franklin joined Collins, he found that his friend had already lost so much money through drinking and gambling that Franklin had to pay his bills. The Governor of New York heard of Franklin's supply of books from the ship's captain, and invited him for a visit; but Collins was unable to go along because he was too intoxicated. The occasion, however, was important to Franklin, because "this was the second Governor who had done me the Honour to take Notice of me, which to a poor Boy like me was very pleasing." Collins and Franklin proceeded to Philadelphia, picking up Vernon's money en route. But Collins borrowed most of it, which he never repaid, and which Franklin worried about ceaselessly, for fear Vernon would ask for it back. Franklin considered his loaning out another man's money another of the "great Errata of my Life."

Collins was unable to find work, but continued to live at Franklin's expense, and to drink. Soon the two began to quarrel.

Then, while boating, the intoxicated Collins refused to row, and Franklin refused to row him. Collins threatened to throw Franklin overboard, but when he approached was himself tossed over. Keeping the boat just out of reach, Franklin kept asking whether Collins would row, and Collins kept refusing until he grew thoroughly tired. He was finally taken back in the boat, but the incident strained their friendship so seriously that Collins went to Barbados as a tutor and never contacted Franklin again.

Governor Keith offered to set Benjamin up in business and suggested that Franklin choose his own equipment in England. So Franklin prepared to leave on the annual ship to London, meanwhile living pleasantly. He was constantly in the company of Keimer, his employer, who loved to argue; but Benjamin so deftly used his Socratic method that Keimer would hardly answer the most common question without asking first, "What do you intend to infer from that?" Keimer respected Franklin's argumentative powers enough to propose that they together establish a new religious sect: Keimer would preach the doctrines and Franklin would answer the critics. But Franklin refused to cooperate unless he could contribute some doctrines, too. For example, Franklin would agree with Keimer that no man should cut his beard, and that Saturday should be observed as the Sabbath, on the condition that nobody should eat animal food. Since Keimer was a glutton, Franklin decided to divert himself by "half-starving him." Both agreed to try the new diet, which suited Franklin because it was cheap. When Keimer could stand it no longer, however, he ordered a dinner of roast pig, to which he invited Benjamin and two ladies. But the pig was set on the table too soon, and Keimer devoured the meal before his guests could arrive.

Franklin successfully courted Miss Read, but her mother persuaded the two eighteen-year-olds not to become engaged until after his return from abroad. He also had three close male friends—Charles Osborne, Joseph Watson, and James Ralph— all readers and writers of poetry. Ralph, especially, wished to be a poet, though the others discouraged him. As for Franklin, "I approv'd the amusing one's self with Poetry now and then, so far as to improve one's Language, but no farther." Once each agreed to write a poetic version of the Eighteenth Psalm. Sure that his version would be attacked unfairly, Ralph persuaded

Franklin to present it as if it were his own. Osborne declared it an improvement over the original and attacked Ralph for criticizing it. This incident, over which Osborne was later teased, convinced Ralph to become a poet. Franklin ends his account of the group by saying that Watson died in his arms a few years later, and Osborne became a rich lawyer in the West Indies, but died young: "He and I had made a serious Agreement, that the one who happen'd first to die, should if possible make a friendly Visit to the other, and acquaint him how he found things in that Separate State. But he never fulfill'd his Promise."

DISCUSSION

This section shows Franklin at his most light-hearted, and contains some of the most admired passages in the *Autobiography*. Portraying the life of a young Philadelphian, it is a good record of the ways in which young people of the day amused themselves, as well as of the shrewdly good-humored young Benjamin. Among other things, it suggests that the love of literature among the colonists was great enough to make James Ralph determine to live by his poetry—at least "till Pope cured him" by ridiculing him in the *Dunciad*. The character sketches of Franklin's churlish brother James and of Keimer have been highly praised for their compact vividness. Keimer's gluttonous consumption of an entire roast pig, for example, has been cited not only for its inherent humor but also because Keimer appears so thoroughly individualized a character.

QUESTION

How different from the activities of today's young men are Franklin's concerns as an eighteen-year-old?

SECTION 5

SYNOPSIS: The First Trip to England

Governor Keith frequently entertained Franklin, always mentioned backing him in business, and proposed that Franklin take letters of credit with him to buy supplies in England. Franklin often called for the letters, but found they were never ready. When his ship was about to sail, Franklin was told that the letters would be delivered to him on shipboard. When Colonel French, a close friend of the Governor's, came aboard with letters, Franklin assumed his were included. The Captain made a check impossible, however, by stating that no letters could be sorted or delivered until the ship reached England.

Having said good-bye to his friends and "interchang'd some Promises with Miss Read," Franklin left Philadelphia accompanied by his friend James Ralph, who ostensibly went abroad to arrange for goods to sell. Because a lawyer and his son were prevented from sailing at the last minute, Franklin and Ralph were invited to travel in the ship's cabin. The trip was marred by rough weather, but valuable in fostering Franklin's friendship with a Quaker merchant named Denham, who later became his adviser in England.

As they approached London, Franklin looked through the bag of letters but found none bearing his name. From the handwriting, and from the addresses to a stationer and a printer, however, he identified several which he felt must be on his behalf, and personally delivered one. But the stationer receiving it asserted that he had never heard of Governor Keith and that the letter was from a rascal named Riddlesden. He then put it back into Franklin's hand and turned away. The letter suggested that a scheme was afloat, in which Keith was implicated along with Riddlesden, to hurt the interests of Andrew Hamilton, a famous Philadelphia lawyer. To revenge himself on Keith for the "pitiful Tricks" played "so grossly on a poor ignorant Boy," when Hamilton arrived in England, Franklin visited him and gave him the letter.

Meanwhile Denham advised Franklin to get a job, learn what he could from English printers, and save his money to get home again. Denham added that nobody ever believed promises Keith made, since Keith "wish'd to please every body; and having little to give, he gave Expectations."

Franklin and Ralph took inexpensive lodgings together, and Ralph confided that he planned to desert his Philadelphia wife and child. Though Franklin quickly found work in a printing-house, Ralph was unable to get suitable employment. Together, the two spent most of Franklin's wages on plays and amusements, and both conveniently forgot the women back home. Franklin wrote Miss Read only once to say he would not return soon, a lapse he considered "another of the great Errata of my Life." Ralph soon established a liaison with a young milliner, and the two moved into other lodgings. Then, since her earnings could not support the two of them plus her child, Ralph decided to become a provincial schoolteacher—a profession he considered so far beneath him that he assumed Franklin's name for the job. Meanwhile, the milliner, who had lost her friends and business because of Ralph, became dependent on Franklin for small loans. Franklin made improper advances to her which she indignantly reported to Ralph, who considered Franklin's conduct sufficiently reprehensible to cancel all past debts. Franklin believed that his behavior toward Ralph's lady constituted an erratum, but felt well rid of so costly a friendship.

Benjamin was composing type for an edition of Wollaston's *Religion of Nature* when he decided that certain passages contained specious reasoning, and he wrote and printed a pamphlet attacking the work (another erratum). His employer thereupon decided he was an ingenious young man, though of abominable principles. But a surgeon named Lyons read the pamphlet, sought Franklin out, and later introduced him into prominent London intellectual circles.

Franklin was known among his fellow workmen for his exceptional strength and his habit of drinking water instead of beer. Though he ran into some temporary trouble when he refused to pay a standard fee twice after being transferred from press work to the composing room, Franklin got along well with his fellows and was soon popular enough to be able to institute various reforms among them. For one, he convinced a number to substitute a nourishing breakfast for their morning beer. And because he never celebrated the weekend so riotously that he was sick Monday, the owner also liked him. After a while he grew friendly with a young man named Wygate, who was better educated than most printers, and whom Franklin taught to swim. In the company of Wygate's gentlemen friends, Franklin performed such remarkable swimming feats in the Thames that word of him spread to a nobleman, who wanted Franklin to give his sons swimming lessons. But by this time Franklin was ready to return home.

The merchant Denham advised Franklin against a proposed scheme of traveling over Europe with Wygate, and instead offered him a job as clerk and manager of Denham's Philadelphia store. Franklin decided to accept the offer, since Mr. Denham promised to set him up in business if he did well at his duties. Franklin knew Denham to be scrupulously honest: having failed in England and left debts there, Denham went to America and quickly made a fortune; he then returned, invited all his old creditors to a dinner, and placed under their plates checks for all he owed them plus interest.

DISCUSSION

The pamphlet Franklin wrote answering William Wollaston's *The Religion of Nature Delineated* argued against the existence of free will, explaining human behavior as the result of a desire to experience pleasure and avoid pain. It also argued against the idea of an afterlife. Wollaston's work, on the other hand, asserted that nature itself provided the logical support for most traditional and orthodox beliefs. Franklin dedicated the hundred copies of his tract, entitled *A Dissertation on Liberty and Necessity, Pleasure and Pain,* to James Ralph, but burned most of them after distributing a few copies. He decided that writing and printing the pamphlet was an erratum because of its possible bad effect on others.

QUESTION

What evidence suggests that Franklin might have prospered equally had he remained in England?

SECTION 6

SYNOPSIS: Preparations to Enter Business

After using the voyage home to devise a plan for his conduct which he "pretty faithfully adhered to" through old age, Franklin arrived to find things changed in Philadelphia. Keith was no longer governor and "seem'd a little asham'd" when encountered on the street. Franklin felt he himself would have been equally ashamed before Miss Read, had she not married in his absence. But she had since left her husband, who then ran away to the West Indies and died. Keimer, on the contrary, seemed, with better equipment, more business, and more helpers, to be prospering.

Franklin soon grew expert at selling merchandise in Denham's store. The two lived together amiably for about four months, until both became seriously ill. Only Franklin evenually recovered. Denham willed him a small legacy, and left him "once more to the wide World."

At this point Keimer offered Franklin large yearly wages to manage his printing-house. Though Franklin wanted no more to do with the man, he accepted the offer because he found no other work. He discovered that Keimer planned to fire him as soon as he had trained the other five workers properly, but he nevertheless did his job well. The men liked him and respected his knowledge of printing. Franklin invented a method of replacing damaged type and could also engrave, make ink, and serve as warehouseman. But as he shared his knowledge with the others, his services became expendable. So Keimer first began to hint that he should take a cut in wages, then grew increasingly quarrelsome. Presently a trifle caused a rupture between them: Franklin heard a noise and stuck his head out of the window to see what had happened. Outside, Keimer saw him, yelled for him to mind his own business, and Franklin quit, feeling he had been publicly embarrassed.

One of Keimer's workers, Hugh Meredith, came to Franklin and reminded him that Keimer's debts and bad judgment would inevitably ruin him soon. Then Meredith proposed that the two establish a partnership in a printing-house: Meredith's father would furnish the capital if Franklin would furnish the expertise, and they would share the profits equally. They decided to set up business the following spring, when Meredith's contract with Keimer would run out. Meanwhile they ordered equipment from England.

In a few days Keimer had a chance to print paper money for New Jersey, a lucrative commission requiring skills which only Franklin possessed. Keimer therefore tried to rehire Franklin, and Meredith persuaded him to consent, since he could teach Meredith more that way. To print the bills, Franklin and

Keimer moved to Burlington for three months, where the New Jersey Assembly closely supervised the business. The committee members appointed to oversee the work were constantly present. They liked Franklin, entertained him in their homes, and introduced him to their friends. Thus life was pleasant and "these Friends were afterwards of great Use" to Franklin, who said of them, "They all continued their Regard for me as long as they lived."

Franklin also describes his beliefs at this time. While his parents had taught him "religious Impressions," he had become at the age of fifteen "a thorough Deist." He had also "perverted some others, particularly Collins and Ralph." But summing up the conduct of the freethinkers he knew—Collins's, Ralph's, Keith's, and his own toward Vernon and Miss Read—he "began to suspect that this Doctrine tho' it might be true, was not very useful." He grew more tolerant of traditional religion because of its morality. Not having had the restraints of these conventional ethics, however, he felt lucky to have survived many youthful hazards. "I had therefore a tolerable Character to begin the World with, I valued it properly, and determin'd to preserve it."

When their type arrived from London, Meredith and Franklin left Keimer before he heard of their plans. They rented a house, the costs of which were cut by subletting part of it to a glassworker's family, with whom they boarded. They had just finished setting up their equipment when a friend brought in a countryman who had been looking for a printer. This first job paid five shillings, which "coming so seasonably, gave me more Pleasure than any Crown I have since earn'd." Franklin felt so grateful that he always tried after that to help beginners.

DISCUSSION

This section, as others, suggests the great amount of time Franklin spent thinking through his religious beliefs. Even when mentioning how his convictions differed from those of colonial Christians, Franklin suggests the importance such convictions had for him. Interestingly, his beliefs center around the proper conduct for daily life; the matters which he felt most important of all were "Truth, Sincerity, and Integrity in Dealings between Man and Man." Franklin later refined his religious convictions, but they remained mainly a set of ethics to govern man's earthly behavior. He never seemed much concerned about a possible afterlife. But his tolerance for other religious systems grew; his convictions grew that the best systems were the most useful systems, and that any religion which fostered moral conduct should be respected.

QUESTION

How does Franklin's stay in Burlington illustrate the extremely fluid and democratic society of the Colonies?

SECTION 7

SYNOPSIS: First Prosperity

After his return from England, Franklin had organized his ten most intelligent friends into a "Club for mutual Improvement" called the "Junto." Each member in turn was required to lead a discussion on morals, politics, or natural philosophy, and to write an essay every three months. The club had firm rules against members abrasively contradicting each other, and against anything which might create personal antagonisms.

One benefit of Franklin's club was that each member helped the new printers to find business. And once he received a commission, Franklin worked so late at night to finish it that his neighbors began to talk of his industry. He was always careful to appear as industrious as he was, dressed plainly, and wheeled his supplies himself through the streets in a wheelbarrow. When a former worker of Keimer's came asking for a job, Franklin foolishly confided his plans to start a newspaper. The man told Keimer, who immediately began his own news sheet. Franklin so resented this interference that he anonymously wrote several amusing pieces which helped Bradford's paper and ridiculed Keimer's. But Keimer published a paper for nine months, after which he sold the enterprise to Franklin for a trifle.

The paper soon proved very profitable to Franklin. He used better type and printed the articles more carefully than Bradford. Moreover, the first edition discussed a current dispute between Governor Burnet and the Massachusetts Assembly that gained subscriptions from everyone mentioned. Franklin furnished examples of his superior workmanship to the Pennsylvania Assembly, too, which voted him Assembly printer for the next year. In this lobbying, a powerful ally was Mr. Hamilton, the lawyer Franklin had warned against Keith's schemes in London.

About this time, Vernon finally asked for his debt, and after a little longer, Franklin repaid it. So he felt one erratum was partially corrected. Then another financial demand almost ruined him. Meredith's father had promised to pay not only an initial sum for their equipment, but also a second hundred pounds after a year. When the time for the second payment came, however Mr. Meredith found himself unable to spare the money, and the merchant they owed sued them. Two friends privately offered to advance the amount to Franklin, but advised him to dissolve his partnership with Meredith, who was seldom sober. Meredith agreed to sell Franklin his share, and went to North Carolina.

When Franklin found himself in business alone for the first time, around 1729, the main public issue was a demand for more paper money, a proposal most wealthy men opposed for fear that currency would be devalued and creditors harmed. Franklin wrote an anonymous pamphlet suggesting several ways in which more money would mean more prosperity for the area. The pamphlet marshaled public support, and the bill to print more currency passed the Assembly. Franklin was rewarded by receiving the commission to print the money. This pamphlet, like his newspaper, proved to him the value of knowing how to write well.

As postmaster, the printer Bradford forbade his carriers to transport Franklin's papers and thus made it necessary to bribe the riders. Most of the public, moreover, assumed that Bradford's paper circulated further and was a better place to advertise. This assumption hurt Franklin's business, though he prospered enough to open a stationer's shop and hire two helpers. But he so resented Bradford's postal policies, that he carefully avoided duplicating them when he became postmaster of the Colonies.

Soon trouble arose with the Godfreys, the family who rented part of Franklin's house. Mrs. Godfrey arranged a match between Franklin and a relative, but Franklin asked as the girl's dowry enough money to pay off his remaining debt. After considering this proposal, her parents forbade Franklin to see their daughter, and he suspected that they were assuming his passion would force him to elope. So he made no more efforts to see her, shunned a reconciliation with her family, and thus angered the Godfreys, who moved away.

But Franklin had decided to marry. Upon investigation, he found that he could not expect a desirable wife who would bring a good dowry, because printing was considered a poor business in Philadelphia (Keimer and his successor both having failed). So he finally returned to Miss Read, with whom he set up housekeeping on September 1, 1730, thus correcting another former erratum.

About this time the Junto Club members pooled their books, but then found the arrangement inconvenient. So Franklin set afoot his first proposal to benefit the public—a subscription library, which was established and later imitated in other cities. Franklin concludes, "These Libraries have improv'd the general Conversation of the Americans, made the common Tradesmen and Farmers as intelligent as most Gentlemen from other Countries, and perhaps have contributed in some degree to the Stand so generally made throughout the Colonies in Defence of their Privileges."

DISCUSSION

Franklin's matter-of-fact discussion of his marriage often appears callous to students who do not realize two things. First, it was common in his day for a bride to bring her husband desirable amounts of money or property, and for marriages to be as much business as romantic arrangements. One could hardly expect a man so remarkably shrewd in other matters as Franklin was to be less so in choosing a wife. The second, however, is that his technical relationship to Miss Read was a touchy matter. Deborah Read had good reasons for suspecting that her first husband had already been married in England, but had no way of proving the fact legally and thus no way of obtaining a divorce under Pennsylvania law. She also believed that Rogers had since died but again, could not prove the fact conclusively. Had she and Franklin observed a legal wedding ceremony and then been confronted by a living Rogers, they could both have been convicted of bigamy, whipped with thirty-nine lashes on the bare back, and imprisoned at hard labor for life. The risks of a formal marriage being so great, Deborah Read became Franklin's common-law wife, though their friends always considered the children legitimate.

QUESTION

Why would Franklin have seemed a good financial risk for those with enough money to loan him what he needed?

PART TWO
SECTION 8

**SYNOPSIS: "Continuation of the Account.
. . . Begun at Passy 1784"**

Franklin includes a memo at this point stating that the account he first wrote, of family anecdotes with little public interest, had been interrupted by the American Revolution. What follows was written to comply with advice in two appended letters, and is intended for the public. The letters from Abel James and Benjamin Vaughan urge Franklin to continue his memoirs, primarily because his life will provide a good example for others, especially young people. Vaughan gives many more arguments, emphasizing that Franklin's story should be one of the age's worthiest.

Franklin wrote the second part of his memoirs without having a copy of his first part (though James had sent him his outline), so he begins by repeating his account of the Pennsylvania Public Library. At the time of its founding, he says, this institution was needed because there were no good booksellers south of Boston, and all books had to be ordered from England. But organizing the library taught him a lesson about neighbors: they automatically resist any project which might give one man a slightly better reputation than theirs. So Franklin learned to identify himself only as a representative of "a Number of Friends," and approach others as "Lovers of Reading." He recommends such self-effacement to others working on public proposals; for "the present little Sacrifice of your Vanity will afterwards be amply repaid." If anyone claimed credit unjustly, it would soon be properly replaced. Franklin felt that the library helped further his own education, and he used one or two hours each day for reading. In fact, he reported, "Reading was the only Amusement I allow'd myself." With a growing family, "My Industry in my Business continu'd as indefatigable as it was necessary."

Franklin considered industry "a Means of obtaining

Wealth and Distinction." Luckily his wife was "as much dispos'd to Industry and Frugality as myself," and cheerfully assisted him in many ways around his stationer's shop. In spite of their principles, however, she one day presented him his breakfast bread and milk in a china bowl with a silver spoon, insisting that her husband deserved such comforts "as well as any of his Neighbours."

Though Franklin found some dogmas of the Presbyterian church in which he was reared "unintelligible," he states, "I never was without some religious Principles; I never doubted, for instance, the Existance of the Deity, that he made the World, and govern'd it by his Providence; that the most acceptable Service of God was the doing Good to Man; that our Souls are immortal; and that all Crime will be punished, and Virtue rewarded either here or hereafter." He felt these beliefs represented "the Essentials of every Religion," so he respected every religion, and contributed to the building funds of all Philadelphia sects. He felt public worship was proper and useful, and therefore helped pay the salary of the Presbyterian minister. But he refused to attend the sermons because he felt the clergyman tried "rather to make us Presbyterians than good Citizens." For his own worship, he used a prayer he composed for himself.

DISCUSSION

Most commentators have felt that the style of the *Autobiography* changes for the worse at this point, partially because its writer was fourteen years older and partially because of Franklin's changed purpose. For now, instead of amusing his son and himself with an account of youthful trials and foibles, he was writing to instruct the public. His tone is therefore perceptibly more moralistic than it had been earlier.

In both parts, however, Franklin stresses the value of industry, because he believed that hard work always led to wealth. He realistically saw that scientific experiments and public service required leisure, that leisure required financial security, and that financial security should be acquired as fast as possible, if one were to engage in either scientific or political pursuits. Since Franklin had the wisdom to recognize when his fortune was large enough for his own purposes, he was able to quit working actively when he was only forty-two years old. He thereafter fashioned a career of such remarkable distinction that most contemporaries must have felt his ideas about industry were self-evident truths. Franklin was always willing to achieve the public goals he aimed for at the expense of his personal aggrandisement, so he should be excused any apparent vanity at recommending his methods to others. He had the rare capacity to starve his vanity for the moment, being confident that it would enjoy a future feast. In this ability, as in others, he proved how exceptional he was.

QUESTION

Why was Franklin so proud of helping to establish the first subscription library?

SECTION 9

SYNOPSIS: Planned Perfection

"It was about this time I conceiv'd the bold and arduous Project of arriving at moral Perfection," Franklin writes. "As I knew, or thought I knew, what was right and wrong, I did not see why I might not always do the one and avoid the other." He soon found the task "of more Difficulty than I had imagined," but decided that one's bad deeds resulted from bad habits, and that with concentration one could substitute good habits for the bad ones. He decided that thirteen virtues were either necessary or desirable, arranged them so that the first acquired could help in assimilating the second, and so on:

1. TEMPERANCE: Eat not to Dulness. Drink not to Elevation.
2. SILENCE: Speak not but what may benefit others or yourself. Avoid trifling Conversation.
3. ORDER: Let all your Things have their Places. Let each Part of your Business have its Time.
4. RESOLUTION: Resolve to perform what you ought. Perform without fail what you resolve.
5. FRUGALITY: Make no Expence but to do good to others or yourself: i.e. Waste nothing.
6. INDUSTRY: Lose no Time. Be always employ'd in something useful. Cut off all unnecessary Actions.
7. SINCERITY: Use no hurtful Deceit. Think innocently and justly; and, if you speak, speak accordingly.

8. JUSTICE: Wrong none, by doing Injuries or omitting the Bene-
    fits that are your Duty.
9. MODERATION: Avoid Extreams. Forbear resenting Injuries so
    much as you think they deserve.
10. CLEANLINESS: Tolerate no Uncleanliness in Body, Cloaths, or
    Habitation.
11. TRANQUILITY: Be not disturbed at Trifles, or at Accidents
    common or unavoidable.
12. CHASTITY: Rarely use Venery but for Health or Offspring;
    Never to Dulness, Weakness, or the Injury of your own or an-
    other's Peace or Reputation.
13. HUMILITY: Imitate Jesus and Socrates.

Franklin alloted himself one week to acquire each new
virtue. And in order to see his progress, he made a record book
and gave himself a black mark each time he failed to exhibit a
virtue on which he was working. He also made a schedule for
his day, alloting seven hours for sleep, eight for work, and nine
for planning, reviewing, reflecting, eating, relaxing, and reading.

Though he found that he was "fuller of Faults than [he]
had imagined," Franklin also found that he "had the Satisfaction of seeing them diminish." He was never good at order or
humility; the latter, in fact, had been added somewhat later than
the others because a friend convinced him that he was justly
suspected of being proud. He later learned that "there is, perhaps, no one of our natural passions so hard to subdue" as
pride; he even wondered, had he conquered pride, whether he
wouldn't have been proud of his humility. But he carefully
simulated the appearance of humility, if not the reality of it.
And though he never attained perfection, he still felt better and
happier from having attempted it. He felt, in fact, that all his
past blessings of health, prosperity, reputation and popularity
were due to these efforts.

DISCUSSION

Franklin's plan to attain perfection astonishes the modern
reader for many reasons, among them the assumptions on which
such a plan was based. For our author assumed not only that man
is perfectible but also that the perfecting can be completed fairly
quickly. Franklin assumed that man is reasonable, that through
his reason he can control himself, and that he can resolve, at a
given moment, to unlearn "bad habits" of thought and action

and substitute good ones. He also assumed that what one should do in any given situation, the kind of action "good habits" would dictate, would be easy to identify.

Franklin's view of man lacks the complexity one acknowledges in a post-Freudian world. But if he appears at points intolerably optimistic about human nature, he also acknowledges his failure to attain perfection with a modern, ironic sense of humor which still makes him likable. Having seen that perfection would never be his, he decided that such a condition "might be a Kind of Foppery in Morals, which if it were known would make me ridiculous; that a perfect Character might be attended with the Inconvenience of being envied and hated; and that a benevolent Man should allow a few Faults in himself, to keep his Friends in Countenance."

Franklin always assumed that virtue was worth pursuing because of its practical benefits, not because of some abstract worth. Order, resolution, and industry, for example, he felt would lead to affluence and independence. And once these last two qualities were achieved, sincerity and justice would be easier to afford. His approach to specific virtues was therefore a practical one. In learning silence, he allowed himself to speak what would benefit him, and in learning frugality, to incur expense that would do him good. It is not surprising, when the spirit behind this list is understood, that the original group of twelve virtues includes both temperance and moderation. For Franklin obviously believed that even one's virtues should be cultivated within moderate bounds, in order to foster happiness, and never as ends in themselves.

His questionable world-view put aside, Franklin's list impresses on a purely literary level. His explanatory maxims are models of well-turned phrases: pointed, concise, clear, and memorable as balanced aphorisms. If the list suggests why Franklin is no longer consulted as a philosopher, it also illustrates why he is still admired as a prose stylist.

QUESTION

What commonly applauded virtues does Franklin omit from his list of qualities necessary for perfection?

PART THREE
SECTION 10

SYNOPSIS: Accounts Written at Philadelphia, 1788

Franklin now decided that most strife was caused by self-interested actions, that few acted for the good of their country or mankind, and that a "united Party for Virtue," formed of the good men of all nations, was needed. He jotted ideas on the project from time to time, in one note proposing a creed for party members to ratify which could fit all religious systems. It affirmed the existence of the soul and of one God who made and governs the world, who rewards virtue and punishes vice, a Divinity who could be served best by serving other men. Franklin thought his sect should be started secretly among young, single men who would submit to a thirteen-week course in acquiring virtues, as Franklin himself had done. This Society of the Free and Easy should consist of members free from debt as well as vice, and its members should help each other through promoting one another's interests and businesses. Franklin concludes, "I was not discourag'd by the seeming Magnitude of the Undertaking, as I have always thought that one Man of tolerable Abilities may work great Changes, and accomplish great Affairs among Mankind, if he first forms a good Plan, and, cutting off all Amusements or other Employments that would divert his Attention, makes the Execution of that same Plan his sole Study and Business."

In 1732 Franklin published his first *Almanac* under the name of Richard Saunders. He continued this publication for twenty-five years, selling nearly ten thousand copies a year. Franklin considered it "a proper Vehicle for conveying Instruction among the common People, who bought scarcely any other Books." Its proverbs mostly "inculcated Industry and Frugality, as the Means of procuring Wealth and thereby securing Virtue." The Preface for the 1757 edition, combining proverbs of many nations, was reprinted in England, on the Continent, translated twice into French, and widely distributed by American clergymen.

Franklin also considered his newspaper a "Means of Communicating Instruction." He carefully excluded libelous attacks and personal abuse, answering those angry writers who pleaded for freedom of the press that he would print their comments separately. But he felt he had "contracted with my Subscribers to furnish them with what might be either useful or entertaining" and therefore refused to "fill their Papers with private Altercation."

In 1733 Franklin helped one of his employees set up a printing business in Charleston, South Carolina, paying a third of the man's expenses in exchange for a third of his profit. When the man died, his Dutch widow managed the business so efficiently and sent Franklin such exact accounts, that he was convinced American women should be given the same kind of education as men: such skills would be far more useful to them in widowhood than the music and dancing they were presently taught.

A preacher named Hemphill arrived in Philadelphia in 1734 and delivered many excellent sermons which Franklin admired. When orthodox Presbyterians began attacking him, Franklin led his defense. But someone discovered that Hemphill was memorizing and preaching other people's sermons. While Franklin found this idea sound, feeling it better to deliver a good sermon of another's than a bad sermon of one's own, Hemphill was forced to leave town.

About this time Franklin acquired a reading knowledge of French and began studying Italian. He agreed with a chess partner who was also studying Italian that whoever won a game would give the other a grammar assignment. "We thus beat one another into that Language," Franklin later recalled. After learning to read Spanish too, Franklin found that Latin was easy. He thus concluded that the order in which languages were taught should be reversed; Latin was easy to learn after French, and those who never got to Latin would still have acquired a usable language for their labors.

After ten years' absence, Franklin returned to Boston and was reconciled with his brother. James felt his death near and asked Benjamin to train his son as a printer. Franklin educated the boy at a school, as well as at a trade, thus amending his early erratum in depriving his brother of several years' service. One of Franklin's own sons died of smallpox in 1736, leading the father to urge vaccination for other children.

The Junto proved so genial a club that many members wished to introduce their friends into the group. Because the membership ceiling was set at twelve, Franklin proposed that each member form another club, without letting that group know of its relationship to the Junto. By means of these subsidiary clubs, the Junto members not only kept in closer touch with popular sentiment, but also found it possible to promote their businesses more widely and to affect public policy through larger channels of influence.

DISCUSSION

Franklin's project to form a party of the world's virtuous men follows logically from his program to perfect himself. Once he assumed that he could become thoroughly virtuous by an exercise of will, he naturally thought of what could be accomplished by uniting those like himself. And he saw no reason to limit such good by national boundaries. With his boundless confidence in himself, he could place boundless confidence in men generally. Franklin always assumed that what was best for the individual would in the long run be best for the mass. And reflecting the needs of his society, he further assumed that what was good for business was good for the country and finally, for the world. He therefore saw no reason why nations couldn't cooperate to promote their mutual self-interest, as long as their good-hearted citizens were so organized that they could be shown where that interest lay.

QUESTION

What probable reaction would meet Franklin's proposal for a United Party for Virtue, if presented today?

SECTION 11

SYNOPSIS: First Involvements with Public Affairs

"My first Promotion," Franklin says, "was my being chosen

in 1736 Clerk of the General Assembly." He was unchallenged his first year in office, but his second year began with an Assembly member's long speech opposing him. Since Franklin valued this job not only for the salary but also for the opportunity it gave him to secure printing orders, he took steps to win over his opponent: he asked to borrow a book, then returned it with many thanks. Being asked for this favor flattered the man, who remained Franklin's ally ever after. Franklin found it more profitable to remove enmity than to resent it, and further observed that "he that has once done you a Kindness will be more ready to do you another, than he whom you yourself have obliged." The next year Franklin replaced Bradford as Postmaster, and found this job advantageous, too, despite its small salary, because it encouraged subscribers and advertisers for his newspaper and made newsgathering easier. Bradford had lost his job by keeping inexact accounts, an error against which Franklin warns others.

The first public affair on which Franklin concentrated was regulating the night watch. The constable of each ward profited from the six-shilling fee each householder paid for a substitute to keep watch. The constable spent many nights drinking with unsavory company instead of walking rounds. Furthermore, Franklin felt these fees were unfair, since a poor widow had to pay as much for her nighttime protection as the wealthiest merchant. Franklin felt regular watchmen should be hired and paid from fees based on the value of the property they protected. The plan was presented at both the Junto and its subsidiary clubs as if it had originated in each group. Some years later, after the various club members had grown prominent, Franklin's proposal was passed by the city.

Franklin also read in the Junto a paper on careless accidents causing household fires, and how to prevent them. Following the Junto's discussions, a fire company was organized which ultimately included most property owners of Philadelphia. Franklin was proud that the Union Fire Company still existed at the time he wrote, though all the original members but two were dead. He was also proud that Philadelphia's efficient fire-fighting system prevented more than two houses from ever being lost at a time.

In 1739 the Reverend Whitefield arrived in Philadelphia to preach, but the clergy refused him the use of their churches. He therefore preached in the fields, where huge crowds gathered to hear him. Franklin used Whitefield's outdoor sermons to estimate that thirty thousand might possibly hear him simultaneously, and to verify for himself the possible truth of historical accounts that generals had harangued whole armies. Franklin observed that Whitefield's older sermons were so well-practiced and modulated that they resembled "an excellent Piece of Music" and concluded that an itinerant preacher had some definite advantages over one who could not rehearse his sermons. Soon money was collected for a meeting house where Whitefield and any other preacher of any persuasion might preach if he wished, "so that even if the Mufti of Constantinople were to send a Missionary to preach Mahometanism to us, he would find a Pulpit at his Service."

Whitefield traveled through the Colonies to Georgia, where the first settlers had been largely "broken Shopkeepers and other insolvent Debtors" who perished in large numbers, leaving many orphans. He soon decided to establish an orphanage in Georgia, and returned north to raise funds. Since he ignored Franklin's advice to bring the children north instead, Franklin refused to contribute, though Whitefield's eloquence later moved him to empty his pockets.

Though Whitefield's prayers for Franklin's conversion were never answered, Franklin had great respect for Whitefield's personal integrity, and remained Whitefield's friend until the man died. Once Franklin invited Whitefield to stay with him, and Whitefield thanked him for "that kind Offer for Christ's sake." Franklin replied, "Don't let me be mistaken; it was not for Christ's sake but for your sake." But finally Whitefield came to grief over his writing, which critics could attack more easily than his spoken sermons. Franklin felt his influence would have been greater had he never written, since his admirers could then "feign for him as great a Variety of Excellencies, as their enthusiastic Admiration might wish him to have possessed."

At this time Franklin's printing business and his unrivalled newspaper were making him wealthier each day. He thus began, on a partnership basis, to establish his trusted workmen in their own businesses in neighboring colonies. The contracts and partnerships worked out well for all.

DISCUSSION

Franklin felt it unnecessary to identify the Reverend George Whitefield of England except by his last name, for he assumed the famous evangelist would be familiar to all. Whitefield's reputation rested on his open-air preaching throughout England and the American colonies. Along with Jonathan Edwards in New England, he began the Great Awakening, the wave of evangelical religious fervor which swept the colonies. As the bemused Franklin records, his eloquence and influence were great, even among those (such as Franklin) who were skeptical of his message and his methods. Whitefield assured the crowds that they were "half Beasts and half Devils," yet still they flocked to hear him. Indeed, "it seem'd as if all the World were growing religious." It is an indication of Franklin's genuinely tolerant religious spirit that though he never subscribed to any of the doctrines Whitefield was promulgating, he still remained the man's close personal friend. In fact, the hall Franklin helped erect for the use of Whitefield and any other itinerant preacher who wished to address a crowd, bespeaks a religious tolerance as rare in colonial days as it has proved to be in later times.

QUESTION

Considering the projects in which Franklin first became involved, what kind of matters apparently captured his imagination?

SECTION 12

SYNOPSIS: A Militia and a College

Though otherwise satisfied, Franklin found two deficiencies in Pennsylvania: it had no militia and no college. In 1743 he therefore drew up a proposal for an academy, but laid the plan aside when he found his intended president was unavailable. He did successfully organize a philosophical society in 1744, but his major challenge was establishing a militia.

The Pennsylvania Assembly was dominated by Quakers committed to non-violence. Since they refused to raise funds for arms, and since fighting between England, France, and Spain seemed to endanger the colonies, Franklin settled on a volunteer militia. He first wrote a pamphlet entitled *Plain Truth,* stating Pennsylvania's danger and the need for a disciplined defensive organization. At a public meeting held after the pamphlet was distributed, twelve hundred people signed pledges to participate in such a scheme. When the surrounding countryside was contacted, more than ten thousand volunteered. All men furnished themselves with arms, formed themselves into companies and regiments, chose their own officers, and met each week for drill and instruction. Women made company flags, with insignia and mottoes Franklin supplied. Declining the rank of colonel in the Philadelphia regiment, Franklin served as a common soldier.

He also proposed a lottery to raise funds for a town battery complete with cannon. Franklin and three others, in fact, were sent to New York to borrow cannon from Governor Clinton. At first the Governor refused their request, but over dinnertime Madeira began to mellow and ended by loaning them eighteen guns.

Friends worried that Franklin's Assembly clerkship had been endangered by his military efforts. A rival for the job advised him to resign, but he refused and was chosen unanimously at the next election. Franklin concluded that the Quakers were happy to have the country defended as long as they were not asked to fight. Many Quakers advocated defensive wars. Franklin learned a lesson in Quaker politics when his fire company met to vote on using club money for lottery tickets to support the new battery. Of the company's thirty members, twenty-two were Quakers, but only one Quaker arrived to vote. As the nine present waited, Franklin was secretly informed that eight Quakers were gathered nearby, ready to appear and vote for purchasing the tickets if necessary. But Franklin never had to call them in, since no others arrived. He therefore concluded that the number of Quakers who sincerely opposed defensive military measures was about one to twenty-one.

Franklin was actually prepared, had his fire company voted against buying the lottery tickets, to propose they spend the money for a fire-engine, and then purchase a cannon (a kind of "fire-engine"), with the funds. These stratagems were normal in the Quaker Assembly; it habitually granted money "for the King's use," never officially acknowledging that such amounts were used for defense. And when the Assembly had been asked by New England for gunpowder, it had voted to give New England money for "Bread, Flour, Wheat, *or other Grain.*" With no objections, the Governor then bought gunpowder, designating it "other grain."

Another sect, the Dunkers, Franklin felt, were much less likely to become embarrassed over such conflict of beliefs, since they refused to write down their doctrines. They found their convictions changing from time to time, and feared that publishing them would make further change impossible. Their leader, Michael Welfare, conceded, "we are not sure that we are arriv'd . . . at the Perfection of Spiritual and Theological Knowledge." Franklin felt "this Modesty in a Sect is perhaps a singular Instance in the History of Mankind, every other Sect supposing itself in Possession of all Truth." But finally the Quakers, not having left themselves so much doctrinal latitude, began refusing to serve in the Assembly, "chusing rather to quit their Power than their Principle."

In 1742 Franklin had invented an improved stove which he refused to patent. He believed "That as we enjoy great Advantages from the Inventions of others, we should be glad of an Opportunity to serve others by an Invention of ours." Both an American and an Englishman made fortunes by manufacturing the Franklin-designed stoves. But Franklin never contested their monopoly, for he wanted no patent for himself and hated disputes

After peace was declared, Franklin turned again to his academy. He enlisted friends, then wrote and distributed a pamphlet about the idea. Next he set afoot a subscription fund for opening and supporting an academy and raised about five thousand pounds. Applying earlier lessons, he said the proposal was not his own but that of some "publick-spirited Gentlemen." The subscribers chose twenty-four trustees and appointed Franklin and the state Attorney General to draw up the constitution for governing the Academy. The school opened in 1749, and soon found its quarters too small. So Franklin helped them acquire the large building once erected for Whitefield's sermons. In return the Academy discharged the debts of the building, kept available a large hall which any visiting preacher could use, and promised to hold a free school for poor children. Franklin was then placed in charge of converting the building to suitable form for the academy. He had the leisure to do so because he took a partner, David Hall, who managed his business for eighteen years. The Academy finally became the University of Pennsylvania. Franklin was proud that many of her graduates had become "Ornaments to their Country."

DISCUSSION

Franklin's views about his stove suggest another aspect of his easily-misunderstood attitudes toward money, for his stove was one of the most potentially lucrative inventions of its time. It reduced by three-fourths the amount of fuel required and doubled the amount of heat another stove of its size could produce. To form a picture of Franklin without considering the man's enormous public spirit—the kind of spirit that gave such an improvement to the world free, as a way of thanking other inventors—is to fail to know him at all.

And Franklin obviously applied the same inventiveness of spirit to his trusteeships as to his gadgets. His negotiations between the Academy and the Whitefield Hall groups (in both of which he was a trustee) suggest inspired maneuvering. And his solutions fulfilled the best interests of both institutions. He got the Academy adequate facilities at minimum cost, and also liquidated the public hall's debts, guaranteed the continued existence (cost-free) of a facility in which any preacher could address an audience, and secured a free school for poor children in the bargain (which neither institution, if left alone, would apparently have provided).

QUESTION

In how many ways did Franklin help to create proper defenses for Philadelphia?

SECTION 13

SYNOPSIS: Philadelphia Politics

As soon as Franklin disengaged himself from his business to perform his electrical experiments and philosophical studies, other people claimed his time. The Governor appointed him justice of the peace (from which duty he soon withdrew, finding he knew too little common law to serve well), the city corporation first chose him as Council member and then as alderman, and the citizens elected him a burgess of the Assembly. All these honors flattered him, of course, especially since they were "entirely unsolicited." But as the former clerk, he was especially delighted—for the ten years he was re-elected—to be able to make his own speeches in the Assembly.

In the next year, the Assembly appointed Franklin and another member to negotiate a treaty with the Indians. Discovering the Indians' weakness for alcohol, the government representatives forbade selling them liquor while the treaty was being settled, but promised ample rum when it was signed. The Indians received their promised rum one afternoon, and by night were drunkenly quarreling and beating each other by light of a huge bonfire. They "form'd a Scene the most resembling our Ideas of Hell that could well be imagin'd." Next day, three Indian counselors came to apologize and to blame their behavior on the rum. But they defended the rum, too, on the grounds that the Great Spirit had made everything for a purpose, and the purpose of rum was to intoxicate Indians. Franklin felt that rum had actually been responsible for annihilating the Indians' East Coast tribes.

A friend of Franklin's, Dr. Thomas Bond, began to advocate a Philadelphia hospital for any poor who needed care. The novel idea found little support until the man approached Franklin, saying that nobody would subscribe to the project until they heard what Franklin thought of it. Franklin promised his help, and wrote several newspaper articles on the topic. Soon it was apparent, however, that the hospital could not be built without help from the Assembly. But rural legislators felt the hospital would benefit only the city, and further questioned whether the plan had common support. So Franklin induced the assembly to allocate two thousand pounds for the hospital on the condition that the same amount were first raised privately. Many legislators who doubted that such a large amount could be raised voted for this bill as a way to appear charitable without having to spend any public money. Franklin then went to the Philadephia citizens, asking them to give generously and thus double their contributions. The wording of the bill thus influenced both Assembly members and townsmen; and Franklin later stated, "I do not remember any of my political Manoeuvers, the Success of which gave me at the time more Pleasure. Or that in after-thinking of it, I more easily excus'd myself for having made some Use of Cunning."

At this same time a minister named Gilbert Tennent requested Franklin's assistance in raising money for a church to house the remnants of Whitefield's followers. But Franklin was unwilling to keep asking friends for money and absolutely refused, as he also refused to give the man a list of generous citizens. Solicited at least for his advice, Franklin replied, "Apply to all those whom you know will give something; next, to those whom you are uncertain whether they will give anything or not; and show them the List of those who have given: and lastly, do not neglect those who you are sure will give nothing; for in some of them you may be mistaken." Tennent laughed, followed the advice, and raised more money than he had expected.

Though Philadelphia streets were straight and regular, they were also unpaved, therefore muddy in wet weather and dusty in dry. Sidewalks existed near the houses, but no provision was made for cleaning them. Franklin persuaded his neighbors to pay a sweeper to clean their sidewalks twice a week. And since their street was near a city market, all noticed the difference clean sidewalks made, and were more ready to accept taxes for paving the city (thereby reducing dirt). The paving bill Franklin introduced into the Assembly passed after he left for England, and he was later wrongly credited with the idea of adding street lights. He did, however, suggests an improved design for the lamps which made them much superior to London's globes. Franklin's lamps, made of four square panes of glass with a chimney to emit smoke, gave more light, since the glass did not cloud up so rapidly as the globes. The lamps were also more economical, since an accidental blow broke only one pane of glass rather than the whole lamp.

When in England Franklin observed how inconvenient were London's arrangements for cleaning streets, how quickly the streets might be swept, and how practical was a single gutter running down the center of the street (since rain gathering into a single stream could easily wash away mud, whereas two streams on each side lacked force to do more than increase the mud). Franklin wrote up a proposal for systematically cleaning London's streets, which he thought workable because Londoners slept after sunrise, thus giving streetcleaners time for their chores. He felt that so lowly a matter as streetcleaning became important when one remembered the number of eyes hurt by blowing dust on a single day in London. He added, "Human Felicity is produc'd not so much by great Pieces of good Fortune that seldom happen, as by little Advantages that occur every Day." One might make a man happier, he felt, by teaching him to shave himself properly than by giving him a thousand guineas: the man might spend his money rapidly, but the skill of shaving would spare him from waiting each day on barbers with dirty fingers, bad breath, and dull razors.

DISCUSSION

Though many feel the *Autobiography* grows dull in parts written by the older Franklin, this section reveals the continuing undercurrent of humor which even the seventy-eight-year-old Franklin conveyed. His descriptions of the Indian apology are as amusing as his reference to their fate is sobering. One also notices the twinkle of irony behind Franklin's descriptions of horrors to be met in a barber's chair. His ironically obvious advice to Reverend Tennent suggests how the apostle of common sense leavened his apothegms with a smile.

QUESTION

Why did his role in establishing Philadelphia's first public hospital give Franklin such pleasure?

SECTION 14

SYNOPSIS: Colonial Diplomacy

In 1753, having already served as comptroller for the American Post Office, Franklin was appointed along with William Hunter as postmaster general of the Colonies. The two were to be paid jointly six hundred pounds as yearly salary, if they could make the amount from the profits of an office which had previously run on a deficit. The two men spent nine hundred pounds of their own money in making necessary improvements, but after four years were able to repay themselves and to report three times as much postal profit as Ireland made. And during his travels in behalf of the postal service, Franklin had the further satisfaction of receiving honorary degrees from Harvard and Yale. But when English ministers imprudently removed Franklin from office, the postal service never made a profit again.

Fearing another war with France, the colonists in 1754 appointed several commissioners, among them Franklin, to confer in Albany with the chiefs of the Iroquois Indians. While these negotiations proceeded, Franklin presented the Congress of Commissioners with a plan for the union of all the Colonies under one government for purposes of military defense. A committee appointed to study several similar plans reported that Franklin's proposal was best; so the Congress unanimously voted to submit it to the Provincal Assemblies.

The political structure Franklin envisioned included a President-General appointed by the Crown, and a Grand Council of each Assembly's representatives. But the Assemblies rejected the plan because it gave too much power to the Crown's administrators, whereas England rejected it as too democratic. Franklin felt in retrospect that his plan had probably been the best compromise between all interests, and that it would have avoided the Revolution, had it been put into effect. The Governor of Pennsylvania liked the proposal; but its Assembly opponents arranged to present it in Franklin's absence, and Pennsylvania mortified Franklin by voting not to consider it.

Franklin met in New York with the Province's new governor, Mr. Morris, who asked how he could avoid so turbulent an administration as his predecessor's. Franklin advised him to avoid disputes with the Assembly; but Morris loved arguing, so was soon at odds with his government. Though Franklin was a member of every committee appointed to rebut a gubernatorial message or speech, he remained a personal friend of Morris's and dined with him often until he resigned.

The basis of most friction between Pennsylvania's Assembly and Governor was that the Governor, representing the proprietary company which originally owned Pennsylvania, vetoed any bill taxing the vast Proprietary estates. Resenting the Proprietors' unwillingness to share the costs of defending or improving the Province, the Assembly began refusing to pass taxes for any purpose—even defense. When Massachusetts asked Pennsylvania for aid of ten thousand pounds to pay wartime expenses, Franklin devised a means for the Assembly to circumvent the Governor by raising the money without a tax: bonds were sold under the auspices of the Loan Office and paid off with the interest on paper money in circulation, and with revenue from an existent excise tax.

DISCUSSION

Interestingly, Franklin had designed a plan for unifying all the colonies under a central government as early as 1751. When commissioners were appointed to secure an alliance with the Iroquois Confederation of Six Nations, many saw the meeting as an opportunity to work out a broad colonial union. But unfortunately, the danger to the Crown's privileges implicit in such an organization was as clear as was the danger to the powers to lay taxes claimed by the individual Assemblies. Thus, in curtailing some of their powers, Franklin's plan frightened all parties.

QUESTION

Do you think that Franklin's plan for unifying the Colonies could actually have prevented the Revolution?

SECTION 15

SYNOPSIS: General Braddock and Preparations for War

England would not permit the Colonies to unite and defend themselves, preferring to send English troops instead. When General Braddock and two English regiments landed in Virginia, the Pennsylvania Assembly sent Franklin, as Postmaster General, to confer with Braddock about sending dispatches and to tactfully change the General's reported prejudice against the Quaker province. Franklin was able to reverse the General's attitudes by telling him what the Assembly was willing to do for the army. He contrasted the number of wagons, horses, and drivers available in Pennsylvania with the twenty-five wagons of poor quality which the General's scouting parties were able to find in Virginia and Maryland. Volunteering to procure these necessary items for the army, Franklin offered such terms as fifteen shillings per day for a wagon, horses, and a driver, full compensation for any loss, and a guarantee that no driver would be conscripted into the army. He then wrote a long, public letter urging farmers to voluntarily provide the wagons for good pay, rather than have the army seize them by force. In two weeks he provided Braddock with 150 wagons, plus horses and drivers. And after Franklin's urging, the Pennsylvania Assembly also sent extra supplies and horses as gifts for young subalterns who had been unable to afford proper gear.

Franklin used two hundred pounds of his own money for advance payments, trusting the army; but the farmers, claiming that they knew Franklin and not Braddock, demanded Franklin's personal bond for everything promised them. Franklin's services were so gratefully received that he was asked to take charge of sending the army necessary supplies. He agreed, again using his own money, for which he was never completely repaid.

Braddock drastically underestimated both the Americans and the Indians. Thus he ignored Franklin's warnings about probable Indian ambushes, thinking of war only in terms of besieging a fort. His army advancing on Fort Duquesne was slaughtered, and those escaping death fled, spreading panic among the troops left to follow behind. The remnants of the army rested, in fact, only after they arrived in Philadelphia, where the citizens could protect them. Franklin felt that "this whole Transaction gave us Americans the first Suspicion that our exalted Ideas of the Prowess of British Regulars had not been well founded." In contrast to the French, who had marched from Rhode Island to Virginia in 1781 without disturbing any property, the British also plundered farms, ruining many poor families. Braddock was mortally wounded in the expedition, lingered several days before dying, but said only two things: "Who'd have thought it," and "We shall better know how to deal with them another time."

Since Braddock's mission was so disastrous, his high recommendations of Franklin's services went unnoticed. Franklin had asked only one personal reward for his work: Braddock's promise to stop enlisting colonial indentured servants in the army, and the discharge of those already taken. Braddock agreed, but his successor refused even this request.

In their hasty retreat, Braddock's men left their wagons and supplies to the enemy. Frankin's personal bond covered material worth twenty thousand pounds, to pay which would have ruined him. A few farmers sued him, but finally General Shirley authorized the proper payments. And indeed, Franklin had had some inkling of what might happen to Braddock, for he had refused to contribute to a fund for buying fireworks to celebrate Braddock's presumed victory.

Governor Morris had continually asked for taxes to cover the Colony's defense, but had been refused because he wanted the Proprietors' estates exempted. After Braddock's defeat, the colonists' English allies objected to this meanness. The Proprietors therefore offered to contribute five thousand pounds to whatever sum was raised through taxes. The Assembly accepted this compromise and appointed Franklin to help oversee spending the defense budget. Franklin also persuaded them to pass a bill supporting a volunteer militia.

While the military companies were forming, Franklin agreed to direct defenses for the northwestern frontier by raising troops and building a line of forts. He easily assembled troops at Bethlehem, to march to the proposed fort sites. To his surprise, he found Bethlehem well fortified, for he had understood the Moravians who lived there were conscientious objectors to violence.

Franklin divided the troops at Bethlehem into three units, each of which was responsible for building a fort. He then went with the middle group to Gnadenhut, a Moravian village destroyed by Indians, where their first job was to bury the dead. On the march, the January rain made their guns useless; in fact, a group of farmers whom Franklin had armed were massacred at this time because their guns wouldn't fire. But though the rain prevented their working every other day, Franklin's Moravians built a rudimentary fort of 455 feet in a week: with their remarkable industry, they could fell a fourteen-inch-wide tree in six minutes.

Franklin observed that the men were happy when working and quarrelsome when idle. But a chaplain accompanying the group was also unhappy because of poor attendance at his services. Franklin solved his problems, however, by suggesting that he dispense the day's rum directly after prayers. Thereafter everyone came to hear the sermon, and Franklin felt the solution much more satisfactory than compulsory worship.

DISCUSSION

Franklin's hindsight after the Revolution—which he fervently supported—probably made him unfairly severe in describing the British resistance to colonial self-protection. Under any circumstances, the Colonies would have had to rely on extensive English help to withstand French and Indian attacks. And the comparison of English marauders to well-disciplined French troops also suggests the attitudes of the elderly Franklin rather than those he would have held in 1755. After all, Franklin had recently been the object of near idolatry during his last eight-year stay in France. Understandably, he felt warmer toward the French when he wrote in 1787 than he probably had thirty-two years earlier.

QUESTION

What do Franklin's activities in Braddock's behalf reveal about his kind of patriotism?

SECTION 16

SYNOPSIS: The Military Leader and Scientist

Franklin had scarcely got his fort supplied and the frontier farms protected when the Governor recalled him to the Assembly. On his way, he rested at Bethlehem, though he could hardly sleep in a comfortable bed any more. While there, he asked about Moravian customs and was told of their communal life, their practices of working for mutual profits, sleeping in dormitories, and eating at common tables. He found that their church music was good, but their sermons seldom delivered to mixed audiences. Their marriages, arranged by the church elders, seemed to work out happily as often as those resulting from voluntary courtships.

Back in Philadelphia, Franklin found that most non-Quakers had joined a military company. He was chosen colonel of his regiment, and this time accepted the commission. At the first military review, the men accompanied him home and fired several volleys in salute, which broke his electrical equipment. And later, when Franklin was leaving town, his officers escorted him to the ferry, riding with drawn swords. Pennsylvania's Proprietor was particularly offended about this honorary escort, since such courtesies had been withheld from him. He reported that Franklin was trying to seize the Province by force and even tried depriving Franklin of his postmaster's office. Franklin, on the other hand, was embarrassed by such ostentation. But soon all colonial commissions were repealed in England.

Meanwhile Franklin's scientific reputation was growing. In 1746, while in Boston, he had been introduced to electrical experiments by a Dr. Spence from Scotland. Soon thereafter, a London scientist named Colinson had sent a glass tube for such experiments to the Philadelphia Library Company, and Franklin had eagerly begun to duplicate the experiments he had seen, as well as to devise new ones. He then wrote Colinson to tell of the Philadelphia experiments, and Colinson read the accounts at the Royal Society of London. At first these papers were ignored in London, and one—on the similarity between lightning and electricity—was openly laughed at. One reader, however, Dr. Fothergill, pressed for their publication and wrote a preface when they appeared in pamphlet form. The pamphlet, with later papers added, ran through five editions.

Translated into French, these papers strongly offended Abbé Nollet, the royal authority on natural sciences, whose theory on electricity Franklin contradicted. At first the Abbé believed this pamphlet a clever attack by his Paris enemies. When finally convinced that a Benjamin Franklin actually lived in Philadelphia, he published a defense of his theory and an attack on Franklin. But Franklin declined to answer, feeling that he had clearly described experiments which could be duplicated and verified if his work were valid. Soon French supporters successfully defended him, and his book was translated into Italian, German, and Latin.

The Franklin papers grew famous because an experiment which he had suggested—drawing lightning from the clouds—was executed successfully in France and excited the public. After hearing of the continental stir over Franklin's experiments, the Royal Society of London began to consider the papers seriously. They made amends for their former neglect by making Franklin an honorary member, excused from yearly dues. They also presented him the gold medal of Sir Godfrey Copley for 1753, which was delivered at a public dinner by Pennsylvania's new Governor, Denny.

During the customary after-dinner drinking, Denny called Franklin aside and suggested that they could make many mutually advantageous arrangements if Franklin would help persuade the Assembly to pass bills exempting Proprietary estates from taxes. Franklin replied that, fortunately, he was prosperous enough to need no special favors, and as an Assembly member could not possibly accept any; but he promised to champion the Proprietor's measures whenever they were for the good of the people. Denny thereafter made the same demands as his predecessors, with the same results—Franklin became his chief political opponent in the Assembly. But they remained personal friends; in fact, Denny was able to give Franklin his first news about James Ralph, the youthful friend who had accompanied him on his first trip to England and had now become a prosperous prose writer.

DISCUSSION

In 1746 the Leyden jar, first known condenser of electricty, had been developed, and soon afterwards a London scientist had concluded that all bodies contained electricity. Little more was known when Franklin began his systematic experiments around 1749. He first devised with a Junto silversmith an improved method of obtaining electricity through the glass tube or Leyden jar, and contributed much to knowledge about this device. He even devised the first electric battery. But he made more fundamental contributions by viewing electricity as a single fluid and by coining the terms "positive" and "negative" to describe its properties. And while others before Franklin had suspected that lightning was electricity, it was Franklin who designed the experiments which proved it. Ironically, the proof was actually performed successfully in France a month before Franklin performed a similar tes: in America. This historical accident occurred because Franklin felt a spire taller than any in Philadelphia, and to which a pointed iron rod could be attached, was necessary to draw the lightning from the clouds. But before he heard of the French successes, he had thought of using a kite. And soon thereafter Franklin suggested the first practical use to which the knowledge about electricity could be put: the lightning rod, which protected buildings and ships from being struck and burned.

QUESTION

What intervening events might have induced Franklin to accept a colonel's commission in 1756, when he had previously refused one on the grounds that he lacked military training?

SECTION 17

SYNOPSIS: Trouble with Loudoun

Finding Governor Denny like his predecessors, the Assembly appointed Franklin their representative to petition the King about tax grievances. Franklin was prepared to sail from New York when Lord Loudoun arrived at Philadelphia to arrange a compromise between the Governor and the Assembly. Having heard all arguments on both sides, however, Loudoun urged the Assembly to comply with the wishes of the Proprietors and raise their own defense money for the frontiers; he said no English troops were available for the area. So Franklin worked out the compromise for which Loudoun later received credit: that the Assembly would pass the kind of tax bill the Governor would sign, but would state concomitantly that the action was taken under duress and over their strongest objections. Then Franklin was free to leave for England. But Loudoun had the power to decide times of departure for all mail carriers (the only passenger ships) docked in New York; and because of his inability to prepare his letters, it was almost three months before Franklin's boat could leave for England.

Everyone discovered that "indecision was one of the Strongest Features" of Loudoun's character. It was so marked a trait that his meddling with the mail ships disrupted colonial business. Loudoun also permanently delayed to repay Franklin the amount spent for Braddock's provisions. He could not believe Franklin really needed the money, saying "We understand . . . those Affairs, and know that every one concern'd in supplying the Army finds means in the doing it to fill his own Pockets." Franklin felt that Loudoun's 1757 military campaign was "frivolous, expensive, and disgraceful to our Nation beyond Conception."

The ocean passage gave Franklin opportunity to witness a wager about his ship's capacity to travel thirteen knots, or nautical miles, an hour, and to observe that ships behave differently because so many different men, with different experiences and opinions, contribute to a ship's building, loading, and sailing. He recommended systematic experiments to determine the best procedures in each of these steps. On this voyage, his ship was chased by enemy vessels and nearly shipwrecked on rocks, but finally arrived at Falmouth. Franklin reached London on July 27, 1757.

DISCUSSION

No explanations completely clarify Franklin's uncharacteristic diatribe against John Campbell, the Fourth Earl of Loudoun. It is true that Loudoun privately suggested Franklin had made dishonest profits through his management of army supplies. But the Proprietors sent equally damaging public allegations about Franklin from London, without receiving such personal denunciations. While Loudoun did unjustly refuse to reimburse Franklin for money spent on behalf of the government, still Franklin did actually have avenues open by which he could reclaim such amounts in England, once he arrived. Of course Franklin hated inefficiency, which certainly characterized most of Loudoun's operations. But he had been engaged in public affairs by the time he wrote his account quite long enough to be familiar with gross inefficiency: "I then wonder'd much, how such a Man came to be entrusted with so important a Business as the Conduct of a great Army: but having since seen more of the great World, and the means of obtaining and Motives for giving Places and Employments, my Wonder is diminished." Franklin also hated inactivity, which Loudoun's delays forced onto him. He wrote his wife while waiting to sail for England, "I know not when I have spent time so uselessly."

But none of these things explains why Franklin repeated in writing the malicious and unproved rumor that Loudoun was profiting personally from the disruption of colonial trade. Perhaps the only explanation lies in Franklin's exceptional disappointment with Loudoun, after his initial and excellent first impression. Following their first meeting, he wrote "[I am] extreamly pleas'd with him. I think there cannot be a fitter person for the Service he is engaged in."

QUESTION

Why did Franklin not denounce the Proprietors for their treatment of him?

PART FOUR

SECTION 18

SYNOPSIS: Assembly Agent in England

Franklin's first step as Assembly Agent was to visit Dr. Fothergill, who advised him to approach the Pennsylvania Proprietors before complaining about them to the government. A Virginia merchant introduced Franklin to Lord Granville, President of the King's Council, who informed him that the King's instructions to the governors became the colonists' laws. Alarmed at this line of thought, Franklin argued that the right to originate their own laws in their Assemblies was guaranteed to the colonists by the province charter; the King could veto proposed laws, but could neither repeal nor alter a law once his original approval had been given.

Fothergill arranged a meeting between Franklin and the Proprietors which began amiably, with everyone present declaring his desire to be reasonable. But after Franklin had presented the Assembly's complaints, and the Proprietors had answered such charges, Franklin felt there was no hope of agreement. He promised, however, to write down his complaints, so that they could be considered at length. The papers were then given to the firm's solicitor, Ferdinando John Paris, "a proud angry Man" who disliked Franklin personally because of Franklin's answers, written on behalf of the Assembly, to his official letters. Franklin therefore refused to discuss matters with Paris, or to talk with anyone but the Proprietors. Then the firm asked opinions on Franklin's paper from the Attorney General and the Solicitor General, who both delayed answering for a year.

A year later, the Proprietors sent word to the Assembly that they wanted to talk with "some Person of Candour" instead of Franklin, who had insulted them by the informal style in which he wrote down the complaints. But the Assembly ignored this request. It had persuaded Governor Denny to pass a law taxing the Proprietary estates along with others. The Proprietors tried to prevent the King from giving his assent to this tax law, alleging that their estates would be taxed unjustly. But at the hearing, Franklin officially promised that measures would be taken to prevent such injustice. Franklin also argued that paper money based on the assumed validity of this tax bill had already been distributed, and that revoking the tax would disrupt the provincial economy. So the law was allowed to pass, though the Proprietors turned Governor Denny, who had originally signed the law as their representative, out of office.

DISCUSSION

Franklin ends his *Autobiography* with a description of his successful stand against the Proprietors.

QUESTION

How effective does Franklin appear to have been at international diplomacy?

CRITICAL ANALYSIS

FRANKLIN'S STYLE

Franklin believed that good writing was smooth, clear, and short. It is an amusing commentary on the lesser talents of his critics that they have needed so many words—"simple," "clear," "terse," "limpid," "economical," "plain," etc.—to say that Franklin's prose met his personal criteria. The simplicity of the style is so domnant a characteristic, in fact, that the major efforts of some critics are spent pointing out exceptions to the rule. Some versions of the *Autobiography* do contain complex, unclear sentences, for example:

> Having emerged from the poverty and obscurity in which I was born and bred to a state of affluence and some degree of reputation in the world, and having gone so far through life with a considerable share of felicity, the conducing means I made use of, which, with the blessing of God, so well succeeded, my posterity may like to know, as they may find some of them suitable to their own situations, and therefore fit to be imitated.

This sentence was actually revised in the copy of the manuscript which Benjamin Bache made, or at least in the version Temple Franklin printed, to fit the style in which Franklin usually wrote:

> From the poverty and obscurity in which I was born, and in which I passed my earliest years, I have raised myself to a state of affluence and some degree of celebrity in the world. As constant good fortune has accompanied me even to an advanced period of life, my posterity will perhaps be desirous of learning the means which I employed, and which, thanks to Providence, so well succeeded with me. They also deem them fit to be imitated, should any of them find themselves in similar circumstances.

But because nobody can prove absolutely that the improvement was devised by Franklin instead of a grandson, the more difficult version is usually printed. The only warranted conclusion about his style one can draw from such sentences, however, is that

Franklin, like all other writers, lapsed into awkward constructions occasionally as he wrote his first draft. Even the most caviling critics have been forced to the grudging admission that Franklin's prose usually stands up remarkably well when compared to that of his peers, and—exceptions noted—that it is remarkably smooth, clear, and short.

Franklin's personal history is like Shakespeare's histories of England—true in some aesthetic sense more often than factually accurate. But, though Franklin's facts are inexact as often as not, we tend to trust his accounts because of another important stylistic characteristic: his objective tone. His apparent willingness to acknowledge his own imperfections, and his understated accounts of his own triumphs, make him appear a man who keeps as sharp an eye on himself as he does on others. The apparent objectivity with which he recalls but never dwells unduly upon a personal insult, or an attempted bribe, or a compliment, or an honor—this carefully cultivated illusion of fairness —explains a great deal of the trust and consequent admiration the *Autobiography* inspires.

Another pleasing stylistic characteristic is Franklin's willingness to speculate about the emotions or attitudes causing men to act as they did. His summary of Governor Keith—"He wish'd to please every body; and having little to give, he gave Expectations"—is not only a beautifully turned English sentence but also an insightful analysis, without the rancor Keith might have inspired in lesser men. This interest in psychology diminishes as the older Franklin takes up the tale, but it never entirely disappears. Even in the last section, Franklin explains his own motives for insisting on dealing with the Proprietors personally, instead of with their cantankerous attorney, Ferdinando Paris.

Finally, the style of the *Autobiography* delights as a reflection of the man himself. And just as Franklin seemed to many of his contemporaries a kind of ideal man-of-the-world, so Franklin's style also fulfills the literary ideals upheld by the eighteenth century: whether long or short, the sentences are compact, the grammatical structures carefully and tightly controlled to make meaning instantly evident, the vocabulary forceful and direct. While the word is so vague that it covers almost any writing which pleases the reader, most critics end by saying that Franklin's style had grace.

FRANKLIN'S HUMOR

Franklin's humor is so different from that which students may be used to that they are sometimes baffled when teachers speak glowingly of the humor suffusing the *Autobiography*. While certainly present, the humor is marked by understatement and irony, modes of speech most effective when elaborate social rituals define "polite" conversational gambits. Thus the wit is often sly and soft, an undercurrent in the flow of language rather than the major channel.

Most humor in the *Autobiography* is found in Parts One and Three, but the dominant kinds of humor in these two parts differ. In Part One we find more often the confident burgher using himself as a target of his jokes ("my small Fund of Sense for such Performances was pretty well exhausted"), occasionally shaping his phrases so pointedly that we smile ("Keimer star'd like a Pig poisoned"), or employing the air of a worldly-wise philosopher, who flatters the reader by assuming the reader's appreciation of ironic jokes directed against men in general ("So convenient a thing it is to be a reasonable Creature, since it enables one to find or make a Reason for every thing one has a mind to do."). Franklin includes several inherently funny scenes in this section (his own capitulation to the temptation to eat fish while sailing from Boston, or Keimer's inability to withstand the sight of a roast pig), but also makes effective humor from the inadequacies of polite speech (Ralph, deciding that teaching school was a profession which might later besmirch his name, "did me the honor to assume mine"). The humor in Part One is rich, varied, and relatively constant.

Part Three often includes amusing anecdotes, and particularly amusing things Franklin remembers having heard or said in former conversations. But this humor comes more in the form of set pieces. For example, Franklin is the butt of the joke when he tells of Whitefield's eloquence which moved him to contribute to the proposed Georgia orphanages in spite of his resolutions not to do so. But the climax of the reminiscence concerns another friend at the same service, who had taken the precaution to leave all his money at home, out of reach of Whitefield's exhortations. When he asked a Quaker friend to loan him enough to contribute, the Quaker replied, "At any other time, Friend

Hopkinson, I would lend to thee freely; but not now, for thee seems to be out of thy right senses." Another self-contained anecdote is a mail carrier's description of Lord Loudoun's procrastination: "He is like St. George on the Signs, always on horseback, and never rides on." Franklin, in this third part, writes as an elderly man who enjoys recounting a good story, whoever originated it. As one who frequently schemed to obtain military funds from the reluctant Quaker Assembly, he especially enjoys the account of William Penn's secretary, who helped the crew fight off attackers when Quakers were first sailing to America. Later Penn reprimanded the man for engaging in violence, and he angrily replied, "But thee was willing enough that I should stay and help to fight the Ship when thee thought there was Danger."

In whatever the section, Franklin's humor is never boisterous nor, at least in the *Autobiography,* bawdy. He remembered that brevity was the soul of wit, and made his humorous strokes quickly, deftly, and subtly—so subtly, in fact, that those unaccustomed to humor which makes demands on the intellect instead of the emotions sometimes miss it altogether.

FRANKLIN AND THE AMERICAN DREAM

Franklin's works written to instruct or improve the public —of which the *Autobiography* is best-known—all rest on assumptions about the possibilities open to the individual, which have come to be called "the American dream." The essence of the dream is that any man can earn prosperity, economic security, and community respect through hard work and honest dealings with others. That is, work is the avenue through which one reaches wealth, and conversely, any one who works hard and uses his opportunities shrewdly can assume that wealth will be his reward.

This assumption was revolutionary at the time Franklin lived. Most European countries were still characterized by a clearly defined class structure; their political and social institutions militated against dramatic changes of economic status for more than the lucky few. Franklin, the arch-democrat, felt that in the American colonies anyone could fashion his own economic and social status through his personal merits. He preached that the possibilities were limitless for those practicing frugality, honesty, industry, and like virtues.

Franklin's own life was the apparent proof of these assumptions: he had left Boston at seventeen, with only a short period of formal education and the knowledge of a trade behind him, had arrived almost penniless in Philadelphia, and had been able through luck and work to make a fortune and to retire at the age of forty-two. He and his readers chose to believe that such a career was possible for any American. Thus for a century—and even today—students are taught the *Autobiography* in order that they might learn this democratic vision of American potential.

Franklin's *Autobiography* thus becomes an important document in shaping American character, because it shaped American expectations. American school children learned through Franklin that the lowliest citizen was as humanly worthy as the wealthiest because of his potential for earning wealth, and that poverty, like body lice, was disgraceful only if one failed to do something about it. Further, they learned that formal education was unnecessary, since the intelligent could learn by themselves. America was the land of endless opportunity for everyone.

Franklin, of course, only articulated precepts which were generally accepted, or at least generally held acceptable, in his society. He did not originate the world view he expressed. But his immense personal prestige, and his impressive personal example, helped to make those precepts appear as almost self-evident truths to moralists of every persuasion.

Finally, Americans chose to believe Franklin's descriptions of American opportunities because they were so flattering. They told the American of his own worth, and promised eventual reward, however gruelling his present labors might be. They suggested that his country was superior to those in which such opportunities did not exist, and that he was superior to citizens of those less-fortunate countries because he had such opportunities. And, Franklin seemed to suggest, anyone who emulated him closely enough could eventually duplicate his prestige and career. Thus for a century Franklin's words maintained in the United States nearly the status of Holy Writ. His vision has been credited as the inspiration for many large fortunes, and his individualism has seemed the paragon of "the American way of life."

FRANKLIN AND THE SPIRIT
OF CAPITALISM

Representative of the suspicion and occasional hostility with which the twentieth century has sometimes regarded Benjamin Franklin is Max Weber's treatment of him in his classic *The Protestant Ethic and the Spirit of Capitalism.* In this study Weber argues that a capitalistic economic system depends on the unnatural inclination of the workers to increase their productivity. He states that this accelerating productivity does not derive from love of money but from love of labor itself. And further, that love of work, or pride in one's occupation, is instilled most effectively by ascetic Protestantism. The Calvinists, Methodists, and Baptists, Weber felt, shared an ascetic attitude toward the world, a suspicion of spontaneous pleasure, and a conviction that man could best serve God by working effectively at his "calling." That out of this affirmation of work for its own sake (an "unnatural" love to other men who generally work only so hard as is necessary to provide themselves with what they need) came an affirmation of such virtues as honesty, frugality, and caution, which in turn produced the dependable labor force necessary for a successful capitalistic system. Weber went on to argue that though the original religious zeal which produced these attitudes flagged, the attitudes themselves remained. The best spokesman for such secularized asceticism, he says, was Benjamin Franklin. In his pamphlet, *The Way to Wealth,* and in the *Autobiography,* Franklin voiced most blatantly and naïvely his convictions that man should be diligent in his calling so that he might earn money for the good of society.

Those who have carefully read the *Autobiography* will recognize the grain (or bushel) of truth in Weber's argument. Franklin made amply clear that he believed a man's first duty was to tend to his own business, and that virtues such as industry and frugality were the best aids to financial prosperity. If Weber chooses to define these attitudes as the spirit of capitalism, then he builds a strong case when he argues that Franklin expressed that spirit as clearly as anyone who ever wrote.

Those who have read their Weber more carefully than their Franklin have often been repelled by the image of a man so engrossed in amassing profits that he seemed to have little more than the profiteer's mentality. They have forgotten that Franklin desired wealth not with an insatiable lust, but rather regarded it as the best insurance of honesty and independence. Because Franklin assumed that men were reasonable, he assumed that others would recognize as easily as he had when they had made enough money for comfort, and would then turn to more important concerns such as dispassionate scientific inquiry, as he did. Franklin recalled the long hours he had worked when first establishing a trade because he was proud he had been able to leave his trade so early. Hard work, to Franklin, was the most efficient path toward leisure. He assumed all would understand that excesses of work were as unreasonable and undesirable as any other kind of excess.

It has been rather fashionable in the twentieth century to view Franklin condescendingly as the patron saint of shopkeepers, primarily concerned with hoarding pennies and denying pleasures. One need only say that such a view ignores the man's temperament and practice, the facts of his life and the statements he recorded. His range of interests, inquiries, and accomplishments remains unmatched in both quality and variety. The zest with which he lived, the happiness he said he experienced, the skeptical humor with which he viewed himself and others, belie the portrait of him as the secular prophet of a joyless, otherworldly, money-grubbing religion of work.

CHARACTER SKETCHES

Benjamin Franklin

The author, writing his *Autobiography* in his old age, reveals himself to be something of a "renaissance man," skilled in many fields: business, science, public affairs, and diplomacy. He believes in hard work, honesty, and the capacity of all men to improve themselves. He possesses a subtle sense of humor.

Bond, Dr. Thomas

The physician who originated the idea of a public hospital in Philadelphia to serve the poor, whether residents or travelers.

Braddock, General Edward

The Commander-in-chief of forces sent to defend the Colonies against French and Indian attacks in 1755. Braddock ignored warnings about the Indians' usual ambush-tactics and was subsequently killed. His army was slaughtered.

Bradford, Andrew

The best-established printer in Philadelphia when Franklin arrived there looking for work. In his first days Franklin boarded with Bradford, though he was employed by Keimer, a rival. Once Franklin began his own printing-house, however, he and Bradford became great rivals. As postmaster, Bradford forbade his riders to carry Franklin's newspapers. Bradford's father, William, of New York, had originally recommended that Franklin try to find work in Philadelphia.

Browne, Dr. John

An inn-keeper near Burlington with whom Franklin stayed on his first journey to Philadelphia. Browne remained Franklin's friend for life, though Franklin felt that Browne's doggerel parody of the Bible might cause much harm.

Colinson, Peter

A London merchant and scientist who sent the Philadelphia Library Company its first Leyden jar for electrical experiments, and who later read Franklin's papers on electricity to the London Academy.

Collins, John

Franklin's boyhood friend whose superior argumentative abilities spurred Franklin to learn to write good prose. Later Collins came to Philadelphia but found no work, borrowed money Franklin held in trust, and never repaid the debt.

Denham

A prosperous Philadelphia merchant Franklin met on his first voyage to England, who advised the youth when he was left stranded in London. Denham later made Franklin manager of his Philadelphia store, but died shortly afterwards.

Denny, Governor

The last governor mentioned in the *Autobiography,* who once tried to bribe Franklin on behalf of Pennsylvania's Proprietors. Though he had given a personal bond not to do so, Denny himself was finally "persuaded" to sign a bill taxing the Proprietary estates.

Fothergill

A London physician who wrote the preface for Franklin's published papers on electricity and later advised Franklin when he arrived as Assembly Agent to petition the government against the Proprietors.

Franklin, James

Benjamin's brother, a Boston printer, to whom he was apprenticed at the age of twelve. James was imprisoned for opposing government measures and was forbidden to publish his newspaper. He cancelled Benjamin's contract in order to make him figurehead publisher, and soon afterwards Benjamin refused to work for him. James was resentful when a prosperous Benjamin returned from Philadelphia, but the two were reconciled years later when Benjamin promised to train James's son as his own apprentice.

Franklin, Josiah

Franklin's father, who immigrated to New England to find greater religious freedom, and who inculcated in his son a desire to become both prosperous and useful.

Franklin, William Temple

Franklin's son, who accompanied him on military trips and government missions in Pennsylvania and England. Later Governor of New Jersey, Temple sided with England during the Revolution, and therefore estranged himself from his father.

Godfrey, Thomas

Glass-blower, astronomer, and mathematician of excellence, who rented part of Franklin's printing-house as a home and became a charter member of the Junto.

Hall, David

Franklin's partner for eighteen years, he managed the printing-house after Franklin himself retired from active participation in it.

Hamilton, Andrew

Famous lawyer against whom Governor Keith plotted. Franklin accidentally uncovered the schemes and warned Hamilton, who later became one of Franklin's allies in the Assembly.

Keimer, Samuel

Franklin's first employer, who was so personally unpleasant that he was repeatedly ignored by the influential people befriending Benjamin, of whom he was apparently jealous.

Keith, Governor

Governor of Pennsylvania when Benjamin arrived at Philadelphia, Keith signed much excellent legislation but never furnished the money or credit he had promised Franklin.

Loudoun, Lord

Commander-in-chief of the British forces in America in 1756. His vacillations irritated Franklin by delaying the packet on which Franklin planned to sail to England.

Meredith, Hugh

Franklin's first partner, who decided after about a year that he was unfit for printing and sold Franklin his share of their business.

Mickle, Samuel

An old man of Philadelphia whom Franklin labeled a "croaker" because he was always forecasting disaster for every person and enterprise. He warned Franklin that any printing venture was doomed because Philadelphia was about to die. Franklin's wryly ironic portrait of Mickle has been cited as a good example of his skill at portraying character.

Morris, Governor

One of Franklin's English friends whose love of argument

soon led him into trouble with the Pennsylvania Assembly and to a very turbulent administration.

Nollet, Abbé

French author of a theory on electricity whose ideas Franklin disproved and who attacked Franklin in print.

Paris, Ferdinando

"A proud angry man" who disliked Franklin for his tart replies to Paris's messages on behalf of Pennsylvania's Proprietors. He was lawyer for Thomas Penn.

Ralph, James

Would-be poet who accompanied Franklin on his first trip to England and who later became a highly respected prose writer at the Court in London.

Read, Deborah

Franklin's wife, "a good and faithful Helpmate."

Tennent, Gilbert

Clergyman who raised money to build a church for the Protestants whom Whitefield had once converted. Tennent is the only man mentioned in the *Autobiography* whose request for help on a public project Franklin refused.

Vernon

Rhode Island resident who asked Franklin to collect a debt for him in Pennsylvania. Franklin suffered great remorse after he loaned most of the money to John Collins. Paying Vernon back his money was one of Franklin's first triumphs.

Whitefield

Evangelist who triggered the "Great Awakening" in America, and with whom Franklin became personal friends.

Wygate

A friend with whom Franklin worked as printer during his first stay in London. Franklin taught him to swim and considered touring Europe with him.

CRITICAL OPINIONS

No man has shed such copious good influence on *America;* none added so much new truth to the popular knowledge; none has so skillfully organized its ideas into institutions; none has so powerfully and wisely directed the nation's conduct, and advanced its welfare in so many respects. No man now has so strong a hold on the habits and manners of the people. Franklin comes home to the individual business of practical men in their daily life.

> Theodore Parker, *Historic Americans,*
> (Boston: H. B. Fuller, 1870).

[The *Autobiography*] is letters in business garb . . . addressing itself to the task, which in this country is every man's, of setting free the processes of growth, giving them facility and speed and efficacy.

> Woodrow Wilson, Introduction to the *Autobiography* (New York: Century, 1901).

And now I . . . know why I can't stand Benjamin. He tries to take away my wholeness and my dark forest, my freedom. . . . And why, oh why should the snuff-coloured little trap have wanted to take us all in? Why did he do it?

Out of sheer human cussedness in the first place. We do all like to get things inside a barbed-wire corral. Especially our fellow-men. We love to round them up inside the barbed-wire enclosure of FREEDOM, and make 'em work. Benjamin, I will not work. I do not choose to be a free democrat. I am absolutely a servant of my own Holy Ghost.

> D. H. Lawrence, *Studies in Classic American Literature* (New York: Seltzer, 1923).

In fact, the *summum bonum* of [Franklin's] ethic, the earning of more and more money, . . . is thought of so purely as an end in itself, that from the point of view of the happiness of, or utility to, the single individual, it appears entirely transcendental and absolutely irrational. Man is dominated by the making of money, by acquisition as the ultimate purpose of his life. Economic acquisition is no longer subordinated to man as the means for the satisfaction of his material needs. . . . It expresses a type of feeling which is closely connected with certain religious ideas. If we thus ask, *why* . . . Benjamin Franklin himself answers in his autobiography with a quotation from the Bible, which his Calvinistic father drummed into him . . . in his youth: 'Seest thou a man diligent in his business? He shall stand before kings" (Prov. xxii. 29). The earning of money within the modern economic order is . . . the result and the expression of virtue and proficiency in a calling; and this virtue and proficiency are . . . the real Alpha and Omega of Franklin's ethic. . . .

> Max Weber, *The Protestant Ethic and the Spirit of Capitalism,* (New York: Chas. Scribner's Sons, 1930).

Every sort of natural phenomenon enlisted [Franklin's] interest and called forth some ingenious idea. . . .

It has been said that Franklin was not entrusted with the task of writing the Declaration of Independence for fear he might conceal a joke in the middle of it. The myth holds a profound symbolic truth. In all of Franklin's dealings with men and affairs, genuine, sincere, loyal as he surely was, one feels that he is nevertheless not wholly committed; some thought remains uncommunicated; some penetrating observation is held in reserve.

> Carl L. Becker, "Benjamin Franklin," *Dictionary of American Biography* (New York: Chas. Scribner's Sons, 1931).

What has puzzled men most about Franklin is that he turned so often and so easily from one career to another, seemingly from no inner compulsion; and that he refused to be completely serious, even about the weightiest of human concerns. Hence the theory that only when he confronted nature as a scientist was he wholly committed. . . . In politics . . . he passed on not a system but the empirical method which American leaders have generally adopted.

> Verner W. Crane, "Benjamin Franklin and a Rising People," *The Library of American Biography* (Boston: Little, Brown, 1954).

The autobiography is also a uniquely American book. After a life like Franklin's had become possible and could be described matter-of-factly, the Declaration of Independence seems understandable and much less revolutionary. . . . There was in America a society which valued the things Franklin could do well: work hard, write effectively, plan improvements, conciliate differences, and conduct public affairs with popular needs and interests in view. His autobiography records these achievements and values and habits which made them possible, and tells how a remarkable human being used his heritage and created a life on a new, revolutionary model.

> Leonard W. Labaree, Ralph L. Ketcham, Helen C. Boatfield, and Helene H. Fineman, Introduction to the *Autobiography* (New Haven: Yale University Press, 1964).

STUDY QUESTIONS

1. Franklin left Boston at the age of seventeen because
   a. his brother James prevented his getting a printing job in town.
   b. he had gotten a girl pregnant and was fleeing her friends.
   c. he did not wish to join his father's business of candle-making.
2. Franklin decided to return to Philadelphia from England because
   a. he had trouble making English friends.
   b. he couldn't find a job in London.
   c. Denham offered to establish him in business if he did well as a store clerk.
3. Which of the following actions did Franklin *not* consider an erratum?
   a. Quitting work with his brother James before fulfilling his contract.
   b. Trusting Governor Keith to provide money and credit for buying printing supplies in England.
   c. Printing a pamphlet attacking Wollaston's defense of orthodoxy.
4. How many hours a day did Franklin feel a tradesman would work who used his time ideally?
   a. Eleven.
   b. Eight.
   c. Six.
5. Which of the following qualities is *not* among Franklin's list of necessary virtues?
   a. Tranquillity.
   b. Independence.
   c. Silence.
6. Franklin always helped support Christian churches because he thought their doctrines were
   a. true.
   b. infallible.
   c. useful.
7. Which of the following public projects did Franklin *not* advocate?
   a. A tax-supported militia.
   b. An academy.
   c. A city park system.

ANSWERS: 1-a, 2-c, 3-b, 4-b, 5-b, 6-a, 7-c

ESSAY QUESTIONS

1. Describe the uses Franklin made of the Junto.
2. Trace Franklin's personal and public relationships to the various governors of Pennsylvania.
3. State the basis of the quarrel between the Philadelphia Assembly and the governors.
4. Describe Franklin's attitude toward the sin of pride.
5. On what basis was Franklin so alarmed when told by Lord Granville, in 1757, that the King's commands were the colonists' laws?

BIBLIOGRAPHY

Amacher, Richard E. *Benjamin Franklin.* New York: Twain Publishers, 1962.

Becker, Carl L. "Benjamin Franklin," *Dictionary of American Biography,* Volume VI, ed. Allen Johnson and Dumas Malone. New York: Chas. Scribner's Sons, 1931.

Bridenbaugh, Carl and Jessica. *Rebels and Gentlemen: Philadelphia in the Age of Franklin.* New York: Peter Smith, 1942.

Crane, Verner W. "Benjamin Franklin and a Rising People," *The Library of American Biography.* Boston: Little, Brown, 1954.

Farrand, Max. "Benjamin Franklin's Memoirs," *Huntington Library Bulletin,* Volume X (October, 1936), pages 49–78.

———. "Self-Portraiture: The Autobiography," *General Magazine & Historical Chronicle,* Volume XLII, No. 4 (July, 1940), pages 403–417.

Stourzh, Gerald. *Benjamin Franklin and American Foreign Policy.* Chicago: University of Chicago Press, 1954.

Van Doren, Carl. *Benjamin Franklin.* New York: Viking Press, 1968.

———, ed. *Meet Dr. Franklin.* Philadelphia: The Franklin Institute, 1943.